THE UK AIR FRYER COOKBOOK FOR BEGINNERS

150 Delicious & Simple UK-Based Recipes with European Measurements - Dinners, Lunches, Snacks, Starters & Breakfasts

By

Victoria Anderson

© Copyright 2022 Victoria Anderson - All rights reserved.

The content contained within this book may not be reproduced, duplicated for transmitted without direct written permission from the author or the publisher.

Under no circumstances will any blame or legal responsibility be held against the publisher, or author, for any damages, reparation, or monetary loss due to the information contained within this book. Either directly or indirectly.

LEGAL NOTICE:

This book is copyright protected. This book is only for personal use. You cannot amend, distribute, sell, use, quote or paraphrase any part, or the content within this book, without the consent of the author or publisher.

DISCLAIMER NOTICE:

Please note the information contained within this document is for educational and entertainment purposes only. All effort has been executed to present accurate, up to date, and reliable, complete information. No warranties of any kind are declared or implied.

Readers acknowledge that the author is not engaging in the rendering of legal, financial, medical or professional advice. The content within this book has been derived from various sources.

By reading this document, the reader agrees that under no circumstances is the author responsible for any losses, direct or indirect, which are incurred as a result of the use of the information contained within this document, including, but not limited to: errors, omissions, or inaccuracies.

Table of Contents

ABOUT THE AUTHOR 6
  AUTHOR'S NOTE 7
  KNOWING THE AIR FRYER 7
  AIR FRYER VERSUS DEEP FRYER 7
  BENEFITS OF USING THE AIR FRYER 8
  HOW TO USE THE AIR FRYER PLUS ESSENTIAL TIPS 8
  AIR FRYER CHEAT SHEET 9
  FAQS ABOUT THE AIR FRYER 10
  AIR FRYER SAFETY 11

1 | BREAKFAST 13
  1. APPLE AND OAT BREAKFAST SQUARES 14
  2. BACON AND EGG CUPS 14
  3. CHEDDAR AND BACON BISCUITS 15
  4. CHEESE BLINTZES 15
  5. CHEESE BREAD PUFFS 16
  6. CHOCOLATE CHIP COOKIE PUFFS 16
  7. COFFEE MUG CAKE 17
  8. COTTAGE CHEESE PANCAKES 17
  9. COTTAGE CHEESE AND SWEET PEPPER MUFFINS 18
  10. CREAMY SCRAMBLED EGGS 18
  11. EGGS AND SAUSAGE CASSEROLE 19
  12. GRANOLA-STUFFED BAKED APPLES 19
  13. HERBED EGG WHITES AND FETA ENGLISH MUFFINS 20
  14. LEMON BLUEBERRY BREAD 20
  15. LEMON POPPY SEED MUFFINS 21
  16. MAPLE BACON 21
  17. PERFECTLY BOILED EGGS 22
  18. MINI QUICHE WITH BACON AND CHIVES 22
  19. RASPBERRY AND WHITE CHOCOLATE SCONES 23
  20. RASPBERRY TOASTIE CUPS 23
  21. ROASTED ORANGES WITH YOGHURT 24
  22. SUN-DRIED TOMATO AND ROCKET EGG MUFFINS 24
  23. SWEET POTATO HASH 25
  24. THREE CHEESE EGG CUPS 25
  25. VEGGIE FRITTATA 26

2 | SNACKS 27
  1. APPLE HAND PIES 28
  2. BANANA AND ALMOND MUFFINS 28
  3. BLUEBERRY OAT TRAYBAKE 29
  4. CANDIED LEMON 29
  5. CHEESY COURGETTES 30
  6. CHOCOLATE CRUMPETS 30
  7. CHOCOLATE-FILLED DOUGHNUTS 31
  8. CINNAMON TORTILLA CHIPS WITH WATERMELON SALSA 31
  9. CRANBERRY MINCE PIES 32
  10. CRISPY ARTICHOKES 32
  11. EXTRA CHEESY TOASTIES 33
  12. GOLDEN SYRUP FLAPJACKS 33
  13. GRANOLA BARS 34
  14. HAM AND PINEAPPLE MELT 34
  15. HAM, BRIE, AND JAM TOASTIES 35
  16. KALE CHIPS 35
  17. MOZZARELLA AND TOMATO HOT POCKETS 36
  18. PARMESAN WAFERS 36
  19. PASTA CHIPS 37
  20. PEANUT BUTTERSCOTCH BARS 37
  21. PEPPERONI CHIPS 38
  22. PUMPKIN MUFFINS 38
  23. SPICED DRIED APPLES 39
  24. SPICED PECANS 39
  25. STRAWBERRY CHOCOLATE MUFFINS 40

3 | STARTERS 41
  1. BACON CHICKEN ROLL UPS 42
  2. BACON-WRAPPED AVOCADOS 42
  3. BREAD PIZZA STRIPS 43
  4. BREADED SHRIMP WITH SPICY MAYO 43
  5. CANDIED SWEET POTATO STACKERS 44
  6. CHEESEBURGER ONION RINGS 44
  7. CHEESY GARLIC BREAD 45
  8. COURGETTE PIZZA FRITTERS 45
  9. CRANBERRY MEATBALLS 46
  10. CRISPY MOZZARELLA RICE BALLS 46
  11. CRUNCHY CHICKEN STRIPS 47
  12. CRUNCHY PICKLES 47
  13. FETA AND FIG MEATBALLS 48
  14. FRESH CRAB CAKES 48
  15. CHILLI GARLIC BREAD 49
  16. HONEYED DRUMSTICKS 49
  17. MINI PORK SLIDERS 50
  18. MUSHROOMS WITH SAGE AND ONION STUFFING 50
  19. PANCETTA-WRAPPED ASPARAGUS 51
  20. POPCORN CHICKEN 51
  21. SHRIMP CAKE SLIDERS 52
  22. SPINACH AND GOAT CHEESE TURNOVERS 52
  23. THIN GINGER BEEF SKEWERS 53
  24. TURKEY AND CHEDDAR QUESADILLAS 53
  25. WINTERY ROLLS WITH SWEET CHILLI DIP 54

4 | LUNCH 55
  1. BAKED BUTTERY POTATOES 56
  2. BEEF AND PORK BELLY LETTUCE WRAPS 56
  3. BEER-BATTERED HADDOCK WITH SWEDE CHIPS 57
  4. BUBBLE AND SQUEAK CAKES 57
  5. CHICKEN PARMESAN 58

6. CHILI LIME CHICKEN WITH PEPPERS 58
7. COURGETTES AND CHICORY WITH OLIVE DRESSING 59
8. CRUNCHY PARSLEY CROUTONS 59
9. FISH STICKS AND FRIES 60
10. HAM AND CHEESE SLIDERS 60
11. HONEYED BABY CARROTS 61
12. LEEK AND PRAWN GRATIN 61
13. LEMON PEPPER SHRIMP 62
14. LEMON PEPPER WINGS 62
15. MARGHERITA PIZZA 63
16. ROASTED POTATO SALAD 63
17. SAUSAGE, PEPPERS, AND ONION SUB SANDWICHES 64
18. SCALLOPS WITH BUTTERNUT SQUASH SAUCE 64
19. SEASONED RAINBOW CARROTS 65
20. SPAGHETTI SQUASH WITH BEEF AND CHEESE 65
21. SPICY GREEN BEANS 66
22. STICKY SWEET CHICKEN BREASTS 66
23. TURKEY BREASTS WITH GRILLED PEARS 67
24. TURKEY MEATBALLS 67
25. WATER CHESTNUT AND TUNA FISH CAKES 68

5 | DINNER 69
1. BAKED STUFFED AUBERGINE 70
2. BEEF AND VEGETABLE MEATLOAF 70
3. BEETS, ONIONS, AND LEEKS 71
4. BONE-IN PORK CHOPS WITH BREADING 71
5. BROCCOLI PARMESAN 72
6. COTTAGE PIE 72
7. GARLIC BUTTER SALMON 73
8. HERBED POTATOES STUFFED WHOLE CHICKEN 73
9. HOT GAME PIE 74
10. LAMB AND SPRING VEGETABLES 74
11. MAPLE AND MUSTARD GLAZED HAM 75
12. MARINATED BARBECUE LAMB 75
13. PORK AND HAM PIE 76
14. PORK BELLY ROAST 76
15. PORK CHOPS WITH GRILLED PEACHES 77
16. RACK OF LAMB WITH WARM SALAD 77
17. ROAST BEEF WITH ROSEMARY AND PARSLEY SAUCE 78
18. SALMON WITH SESAME MUSTARD DRESSING 78
19. SEA BASS WITH CITRUS-DRESSED BARLEY 79
20. STICKY SMOKED RIBS 79
21. SWEET AND SPICY BRUSSELS SPROUTS 80
22. THYME TURKEY LEGS 80
23. TURKEY TENDERLOIN 81
24. VEAL PARMESAN 81
25. VEGETABLE POT PIE 82

6 | VEGAN 83
1. AVOCADO "EGG" ROLLS 84
2. BANANA AND CURRANT BREAD 84
3. BATTERED TOFU SLABS 85
4. BLACK BEAN BURGERS 85
5. CARROT MUG CAKE 86
6. CAULIFLOWER WINGS 86
7. CHICKPEA AND CAULIFLOWER TACOS 87
8. CHICKPEA BALLS 87
9. CORIANDER AND SWEET POTATO PATTIES 88
10. COURGETTE CORN PATTIES 88
11. CURRIED CHICKPEA POTATO JACKETS 89
12. FRIED TEMPEH WITH PEANUT SAUCE 89
13. GARLIC MUSHROOMS 90
14. GRILLED BOK CHOY 90
15. HASSELBACK POTATOES WITH HERB VINAIGRETTE 91
16. KALE AND POTATO NUGGETS 91
17. MARINATED CAULIFLOWER WITH WATERCRESS PUREE 92
18. MUSHROOM HAND PIES 92
19. PERSIMMON, TOFU, AND PEPPER SKEWERS 93
20. ROASTED POTATO WEDGES WITH VEGAN MAPLE MUSTARD MAYO 93
21. SIMPLE ALL-ROUNDER TOFU 94
22. SOYA NUGGETS WITH ROASTED LEMONS 94
23. SUPREME CRUNCHWRAP 95
24. VEGAN AUBERGINE "PARMESAN" 95
25. VEGAN BEAN BALLS 96

WRAPPING UP 96

ABOUT THE AUTHOR

A group of Chefs trying to make cooking fun and healthy again!

We know how busy you are, that is why we aim to make our recipes as easy, budget friendly and delicious as possible, so you can cook up meals you look forward to that nourish you simultaneously.

With every book we create we also include a Bonus PDF so you get access to coloured images with every single recipe! We couldn't include them in the book due to printing costs and we wanted to keep the books as affordable as possible. We hope you enjoy!

Please email us & our customer support team will help as soon as we possibly can! We want to make sure you are 100% satisfied and if you have any issues at all please email us and we will do our best to help.

Also, if you have any feedback on how we can improve this book & further books please email us that and we will make all the changes we can. As mentioned we can't add colour photos inside the book due to printing costs, but any other improvements we would love to make!

Our customer support email is **vicandersonpublishing@gmail.com** – as mentioned email us anything you wish here 😊

Happy Cooking!

AUTHOR'S NOTE

By now, you've probably heard enough good words about the air fryer and can't wait to start using one. Maybe you've got one seated on your countertop or you're looking to make a purchase; either way, I have good news for you. The air fryer is one of the best appliances I've ever bought, which should give you the needed encouragement to start using yours or purchasing one.

Having taken off the energetic and unhealthy burden that using deep fryers causes, the air fryer proves to be such a blessing to the culinary world. Initially, it was introduced to the market as a substitute for the deep fryer. However, in recent developments, many models of the air fryer have become better replacements for other kitchen appliances all in one. That said, if you're a beginner cook, bachelor, student, or have got a small kitchen space, the air fryer is one appliance that would come in handy for your daily healthy meals. Even as a family person, the air fryer helps me make dishes quicker and with less stress and oil burns. It is perfect for all.

In this cookbook, I share my love for the air fryer with you through 150 recipes that I have enjoyed over the years. They are a merge between simple, easy, scrumptious, and satisfying recipes that I know you'd love.

The air fryer makes nearly anything; hence, for a beginner cook, your options to make more sumptuous foods than heating frozen foods is achievable. With options that span across breakfast, lunch, dinner, snack, and starters, including a vegan section, there's so much to make for many days. Meanwhile, they are mostly straightforward to make, with a few in there to challenge you a bit. However, overall, these recipes are delicious and can be enjoyed every day.

Fortunately, with the air fryer, there isn't much pre-work to be done when setting it up. So, I would say scan through the recipes, pick out your first choices, and let's head over to the kitchen to make them.

I hope the recipes make you smile as you enjoy every single one of them.

KNOWING THE AIR FRYER

Besides counter space being a hot commodity these days, not many people have much time to waste in the kitchen anymore. I hope our grandmas didn't hear this.

The air fryer has quickly become one of those appliances, like a microwave that every household seems to be reaching out for. It walks the talk of creating quick healthy meals with the least fuss possible while being more multi-functional than a deep fryer. Who doesn't want this? So, if you chose to go with the air fryer, then you made the right choice.

Come for a treat as we explore the many functions that the air fryer operates as. In the recipes, I make sure to tackle the different functions that you can use the air fryer for, so that your purchase is worth the investment.

Like an oven, the air fryer primarily air fries foods and will bake and roast as well. But that doesn't end there. Most air fryer models can also grill, dehydrate, toast, broil, and warm foods with ease. Thus, making it such a rounded functioning appliance that could singularly feed you with different foods for so long.

Meanwhile, it is durable and long lasting. Yes, I heard you question its durability. Having gone through several quality checks and development, it is with much confidence that you can grab an air fryer and be sure of its long-lasting use. And many manufacturers will back this up with some kind of warranty. However, you'd need to do some research when choosing the ideal brand that works for you.

AIR FRYER VERSUS DEEP FRYER

In simple terms, the difference between both is that the deep fryer uses several cups of oil for frying, and the air fryer doesn't. This would imply the unhealthy impact that the deep fryer causes and, hence, being the driving force behind the creation of the air fryer.

The air fryer operates a hot air circulation technology that blows over foods in its basket to quickly dry out liquids and crisp foods. It requires a tiny amount of oil for cooking as compared to the deep fryer and does a better job of creating bite-worthy crunch.

The air fryer cooks food at a high temperature with its high-powered fan, which informs its faster cooking than a deep fryer or oven. The deep fryer would rather cook food in a container of oil that must be heated to a specific temperature. Both options are great for cooking foods quickly but because the air fryer operates with more controllable temperatures than a deep fryer, foods are less likely to burn than with a deep fryer when left unchecked. With the air fryer, once the food is done cooking to the set time, it beeps off and ends the cooking process. You don't get this luxury with the deep fryer.

Preheating is essential for most cooking processes including deep frying but the air fryer can cook foods without preheating. It is, however, advised to preheat the air fryer for 5 minutes before cooking to aid its life span. The deep fryer would adversely require at least 10 minutes of oil preheating before foods can be introduced to it.

Because the air fryer is great at drying out foods for the best colour and crisp, it works better with drier foods than ones with a lot of liquid such as dripping batter. This option would work better for a deep fryer as wet batter can easily fry in a vat of oil.

The air fryer is great for cooking solid foods with the least liquid and oils as much as possible. So, when planning meals, you'd want to cook foods that can easily be baked in it. Think meats, casseroles, vegetables, and other solid foods that won't cause a liquid mess in the air fryer.

Technically, all meats that have no dripping batter are ideal. When looking to bake foods with liquids like casseroles and bread batter, contain them in a baking dish or ramekin before placing them in the air fryer. Fish and seafood are also perfect and would cook in the quickest time. Other options like vegetables, nuts, biscuits, and burgers can be cooked directly in the air fryer.

When considering healthier options, the air fryer offers a better approach for healthier cooking than deep frying. It cooks faster, creates better crisps, is safer to use, and prevents a better degree of burning than a deep fryer.

BENEFITS OF USING THE AIR FRYER

By now, my introduction may have dashed out some reasons why you should get the air fryer but let's weigh in a little more on why I think the air fryer is good for you.

It is a healthier cooking option

The air fryer is built around a single notion that using excessive oils in cooking is harmful to our health. Therefore, its technology is based on using the least oil possible when cooking. It uses a hot air blowing technique that engages the natural oils and liquids in foods to crisp it up rather than introducing excessive oils like traditional deep frying. Even to consider that many oils on the market are unhealthy, this cookbook focuses on using olive oil when needed.

It is fast, easy, and safe to use

Using the air fryer is such a breeze, making it a great option for beginner cooks. Again, its hot air blowing technique cooks food in a faster time. It is safe to use and once your food is prepped, you only leave it in the air fryer to do its work and really, that's just about it.

It is versatile

We kind of brushed on this part a little earlier but as it is, the air fryer is multi-functional and would save you extra counter space. Most air fryers go beyond frying foods so that you can bake, roast, reheat, broil, dehydrate, and roast in it.

It is cost and space saving

Because the air fryer is multi-functional, it works as a deep fryer, an oven, a broiler, a microwave, a grill, and a smoker all in one. That is a lot of money and space that you can save up on when using the air fryer.

It offers the best crisps and crunch

Nothing is heartier than the right crunch you get when you bite into fried foods. And sometimes, the deep fryer or oven would disappoint you at this but the air fryer wouldn't. The air fryer's goal is to dry out as much liquid from foods when cooking through hot air circulation. Hence, it creates the best colour, crisp, and crunch on foods when cooked under the right temperature and time.

It is easily compatible with other accessories

When using the air fryer, certain recipes like the ones in this cookbook may require using other accessories that may not come packaged with the air fryer. Fortunately, the air fryer is designed to accommodate them. Examples like baking dishes, skewers, cake pans, trivets, and many others are options that are safe to use with the air fryer. However, when purchasing accessories for your air fryer, always ensure that they are safe to use for it.

It is easy to clean

The hallmark for any good performing appliance lies in how easy it is to clean after each use. The air fryer is one that is seamless to clean, so you do not have oils and food particles clogging it. You can simply wipe away food particles and leave it to air dry. It'll aid its lifespan and help its quality functioning.

HOW TO USE THE AIR FRYER PLUS ESSENTIAL TIPS

Using the air fryer is pretty straightforward and, in most cases, the recipe in question would guide you. However, here are some quick tips to consider when using your air fryer.

Preheat the air fryer: While this option is not mandatory, preheating the air fryer creates a conducive heat environment for the foods you're about to cook. Most air fryers suggest preheating for about 5 minutes before food is introduced.

Do not overcrowd the basket: Packing up the air fryer basket affects the cooking temperature and hinders the operating unit from circulating hot air around the food effectively. Doing this may gradually or instantly damage the air fryer while also not cooking food accurately. Attempt cooking your food in batches as it is worth the patience.

Choose the right temperature: Always work with the right temperature when cooking your foods for the best results. Below,

I share a temperature cheat sheet as a tweakable standard for helping you cook foods right. Also, the recipes are perfect guides.

Check your food as it cooks: It is okay to pull out the air fryer basket after a while of cooking to check foods. This helps you ensure that they are cooking right and allows you to make adjustments when needed.

Use a little amount of oil when cooking: Except for when you're dehydrating fruits and vegetables in the basket, always mist the basket with a little amount of oil before cooking. This helps prevent sticking while aiding crisping. When baking in a dish, you can skip this step or grease the baking dish.

Shake or flip foods as it cooks: For the right doneness for your foods, shake the basket for foods like potato fries or flip foods like meats during cooking. This way, you can cook them well on both sides.

Use the air fryer pre-sets: Most air fryers come with pre-sets to help you cook foods accurately. When not working with a trusted recipe or looking to make adjustments, the air fryer pre-sets are a good option to rely on.

AIR FRYER CHEAT SHEET

VEGETABLES:

FOOD	TEMPERATURE (°C)	TIME
Asparagus	180°C	5 mins
Brussels sprouts	160°C	15 mins
Broccoli	180°C	6 mins
Cauliflower	180°C	12 mins
Corn on the cob	200°C	6 mins
Green beans	180°C	5 mins
Potato wedges	200°C	18 to 20 mins
Squash	180°C	12 mins
Sweet potatoes	190°C	30 mins
Courgettes	180°C	12 mins

MEATS:

FOOD	TEMPERATURE (°C)	TIME
Bacon	200°C	5 to 7 mins
Burger	185°C	8 to 10 mins
Chicken breasts	190°C	12 mins
Chicken drumsticks	185°C	20 mins
Chicken tenders	180°C	8 to 10 mins
Chicken thighs	190°C	22 mins
Chicken wings	200°C	12 mins
Lamb	200°C	12 mins
Meatballs	200°C	5 mins
Pork chops	200°C	12 mins
Pork loin roast	180°C	55 mins
Steak	200°C	12 to 18 mins
Turkey	200°C	12 mins
Whole chicken	180°C	75 mins

FISH AND SEAFOOD:

FOOD	TEMPERATURE (°C)	TIME
Calamari	190°C	4 mins
Crab cakes	175°C	12 mins
Salmon fillets	190°C	10 mins
Scallops	200°C	4 mins
Shrimp or prawns	200°C	4 mins
Tuna steak	200°C	7 to 10 mins
White fish fillet	200°C	10 mins

FROZEN FOODS:

FOOD	TEMPERATURE (°C)	TIME
Chicken nuggets	200°C	14 to 18 mins
Fish sticks	200°C	10 to 14 mins
French fries	200°C	14 to 18 mins
Mozzarella sticks	200°C	8 mins
Onion rings	200°C	8 mins
Breaded shrimp	200°C	9 mins

FAQS ABOUT THE AIR FRYER

Which air fryer should I buy?

While there are many great air fryers on the market, there is no straight-cut approach for choosing a particular air fryer. However, you should consider the size, counter space, and cost when making a decision.

Can I use oil in the air fryer?

Yes! The air fryer requires a little amount of oil that aids in crisping foods and prevents foods from sticking to the basket when cooking. You can mist cooking spray when cooking or rub or brush oil directly on foods before cooking.

Can I use parchment or foil in my air fryer?

Yes, you can. Both materials are air fryer friendly and would help prevent foods from sticking to the basket, catch grease, or help create steam for foil-wrapped foods.

Why does my air fryer smell like plastic?

It is normal for your air fryer to smell like plastic when it is new because of the material that it is made of, which is plastic. Preheating the air fryer for a couple of minutes can help release the new air fryer odour.

Can you cook more than one thing in the air fryer?

This is only applicable if both foods can cook at the same temperature and time. You can also use a trivet to layer foods in the air fryer to cook multiple foods at the same time. However, make sure not to overcrowd the basket to prevent uncooked food.

Can I cook frozen foods in the air fryer?

Yes! Simply use a trusted recipe to guide you.

Can I use a glass bowl in the air fryer?

Yes! Ovenproof glass bowls like ramekins are perfect to use in the air fryer.

Do air fryers use a lot of energy?

One of the pluses for using an air fryer is that it doesn't use much electricity. It also doesn't heat up outwardly to make the room warm.

I followed a recipe with my air fryer and it turned out undercooked or overcooked. What should I do?

Do not worry. Most air fryers operate a little differently from others. The best thing to do is to check your food every few minutes during cooking to ensure that it cooks to your desired doneness.

Is the air fryer better and safe to cook food in?

Yes, it is. It is produced under safe health and manufacturing guidelines and is great for many households. The air fryer is also versatile and can operate many functions like frying, baking, roasting, broiling, dehydrating, and reheating. This multifunctionality makes it more convenient to use than many other appliances.

AIR FRYER SAFETY

It is essential that you read and follow every safety precaution that is included in the manual that comes with your air fryer's package. Here are some quick tips to also help you use your air fryer:

- The air fryer is designed to air fry food using hot air and less oil. Do NOT fill your air fryer with oil as you would do with a deep fryer. It'll damage it.
- Do NOT fill your air fryer bucket with water with an attempt to boil or steam foods. It is designed to dry and crisp foods. Doing this would damage it.
- Keep your air fryer in a well-ventilated area to allow room for enough air circulation around it. Do NOT set it too close to the wall to help the air fryer's exhaust to ventilate comfortably.
- Look out for the types of oils that you use. Avoid using oils with low smoke points, for example, walnut oil as they may smoke, splatter, or burn the heating element. Stick to high smoke point oils like olive oil, avocado oil, and canola oil.
- Always use heat proof coverings to protect your hands and counter space from the hot air fryer basket. A trivet, hot pad, or pot holder are great options for heat proofing.
- Never place your air fryer or any component of it over a stovetop's fire.
- Always unplug your air fryer after use.
- Preferably, clean your air fryer after each use to keep it odourless and long lasting.

SECTION 1.

BREAKFAST

**Don't Forget To Get The Color Images FREE!
Simply Scan The QR Code Below!**

Please scan the QR code below to access your bonus PDF with all 150 recipes with full coloured photos & beautiful designs alongside!

This is the only way we can get the recipes with coloured photos to you & keep the book as reasonably priced as possible.

Also, once downloaded you can take the PDF with you digitally wherever you go- meaning you can cook these recipes wherever you may be! (As long as you have an air fryer!)

We hope you enjoy and do let us know your feedback!

(INSERT QR CODE HERE)

STEP BY STEP Guide-

1. Open Your Phones (Or Any Device You Want The Book On) Back Camera. The Back Camera Is The One You use as if you are taking a picture of someone.
2. Simply point your Camera at the QR code and 'tap' the QR code with your finger to focus the camera.
3. A link / pop up will appear. Simply tap that (and make sure you have internet connection) and the FREE PDF containing all of the coloured images should appear.
4. Now you have access to these FOREVER. Simply 'Bookmark' The tab it opened on, or download the document and take wherever you want.
5. Repeat this on any device you want it on! (If you want it on a laptop, simply email the document to yourself!)

Any issues please email us at **vicandersonpublishing@gmail.com** and we will be happy to help!!

1. APPLE AND OAT BREAKFAST SQUARES

These breakfast pieces make for a great after-workout snack and would energise you in an instance. They are also quick to make and can pass as a midday snack too.

PREPARATION TIME: 10 MINUTES
COOKING TIME: 20 MINUTES
PER SERVING (4): KCAL: 958; FAT: 16.6G; CARBS: 171.71G; PROTEIN: 36.39G; SUGARS: 34.4G; FIBRE: 23.5G

INGREDIENTS:

- Cooking spray
- 1.1 kg old-fashioned rolled oats
- 1 tbsp. ground cinnamon
- 2 tsp. baking powder
- A pinch of salt
- 2 large eggs, cracked into a bowl
- 240 ml unsweetened applesauce
- 120 ml maple syrup
- 1 medium apple, any type, cut into 1.5 cm chunks

INSTRUCTIONS:

Step 1: Preheat the air fryer to 175°C.

Step 2: Mix the oats, cinnamon, baking powder, and salt in a bowl. In another bowl, whisk the eggs, applesauce, and maple syrup. Combine both mixtures well and mix in the apple chunks.

Step 3: Line the air fryer basket with parchment paper and mist the paper with cooking spray.

Step 4: Carefully, spread the mixture into an even layer in the air fryer basket. You can divide the mixture into two and bake in two batches.

Step 5: Bake for 20 minutes or until golden brown and no longer wet.

Step 6: Remove from the air fryer and let it cool completely. When cool, cut the baked oats into squares and lift them onto a plate.

2. BACON AND EGG CUPS

Mini egg cups are great for when you need to eat breakfast on your way out. You can also make them in a few batches for later and simply warm them when needed for an effortless breakfast.

PREPARATION TIME: 10 MINUTES
COOKING TIME: 10 MINUTES
PER SERVING (4): KCAL: 136; FAT: 10.5G; CARBS: 1.74G; PROTEIN: 8.14G; SUGARS: 1.08G; FIBRE: 0.5G

INGREDIENTS:

- Cooking spray
- 2 bacon slices, cut in halves
- 4 large eggs
- 1 small red bell pepper, diced
- 1 tbsp. chopped fresh parsley
- Salt and black pepper to taste

INSTRUCTIONS:

Step 1: Preheat the air fryer to 170°C and grease a four-cup muffin tin with cooking spray.

Step 2: Line the cups of the muffin tin with one bacon each and set it aside.

Step 3: Crack the eggs into a bowl, season with salt and black pepper, and mix in the bell pepper and parsley. Pour the egg mixture into the muffin tins (between the bacon lining, as much as possible but not a rule).

Step 4: Place the tin in the air fryer and bake for 8 to 10 minutes or until the eggs set within and the bacon is cooked.

Step 5: Take out the tin, let it cool for a minute, and remove the egg cups for serving.

3. CHEDDAR AND BACON BISCUITS

These biscuits are a great addition to your breakfast basket. Bake them fresh for a fun time with the family. What's special is that they include salty meaty hints that spice up your morning routine.

PREPARATION TIME: 10 MINUTES
COOKING TIME: 10 MINUTES
PER SERVING (4): KCAL: 642; FAT: 40.35G; CARBS: 52.92G; PROTEIN: 17.21G; SUGARS: 3.38G; FIBRE: 1.8G

INGRENKEDIENTS:

- 450 g plain flour
- 1 tsp. baking soda
- 2 tsp. baking powder
- 1 tsp. garlic powder
- 1 tsp. salt
- 120 g cold butter, cut into small cubes
- 2 cooked bacon slices, finely chopped
- 225 g grated cheddar cheese
- 240 ml buttermilk

INSTRUCTIONS:

Step 1: Preheat the air fryer to 190°C.

Step 2: In a bowl, mix the flour, baking soda, baking powder, garlic powder, and salt. Add the butter to the mixture and mix with your hands or until resembling fine breadcrumbs. Stir in the bacon and cheese. After, pour in the buttermilk and mix until it is well combined but not firm.

Step 3: Line the air fryer basket with parchment paper and use a small knife to create a few holes through the paper to aid air circulation.

Step 4: Using an ice cream scoop, add dollops of the dough to the air fryer basket with spaces between each one.

Step 5: Bake for 5 to 10 minutes or until they are golden brown and puffed up.

Step 6: Remove the biscuits onto a wire rack to cool and then serve.

4. CHEESE BLINTZES

Besides the fact that these blintzes require some patience and time to get done, they are utterly mouth-watering. They are rich with a cottage cheese filling that's such a pamper for the morning.

PREPARATION TIME: 15 MINUTES
COOKING TIME: 20 MINUTES OR MORE
PER SERVING (4): KCAL: 430; FAT: 21.32G; CARBS: 36.64G; PROTEIN: 22.16G; SUGARS: 17.68G; FIBRE: 0.6G

INGREDIENTS:

For the cheese filling:
- 1 tbsp. unsalted butter
- 1 large egg yolk
- 450 g cottage cheese
- 30 g granulated sugar
- ½ tsp. vanilla extract
- A pinch of salt

For the pancakes:
- 3 large eggs
- 240 ml whole milk
- 2 tbsp. vegetable oil
- 170 g plain flour
- A pinch of kosher salt
- Cooking spray
- Icing sugar, for dusting

INSTRUCTIONS:

For the cheese filling:

Step 1: In a bowl, mix the butter, egg yolk, cottage cheese, sugar, vanilla, and salt. Cover and refrigerate while you make the pancakes.

For the pancakes:

Step 2: Crack the eggs into a bowl and whisk with the milk and oil. Add the flour and salt and mix until smooth batter forms.

Step 3: Grease a flat pan (that is safe for your air fryer) with cooking spray and place it in the air fryer.

Step 4: Preheat the air fryer to 160°C.

Step 5: Add 2 tbsp. of the batter to the pan and spread it out widely. Cook the batter for 1 to 2 minutes or until it is set.

Step 6: Remove the pancake onto a plate and continue making more the same way until the you run out of batter.

Step 7: In one pancake, spread 2 tbsp. of the cheese filling along one side. Roll it up like a wrap or burrito and place it aside. Fill and roll the remaining pancakes the same way.

Step 8: Sift the icing sugar on the blintzes and serve.

5. CHEESE BREAD PUFFS

These cheesy bread puffs serve well with scrambled eggs or some butter or jam for a simple breakfast. You can even make a bunch to serve with soup.

PREPARATION TIME: 15 MINUTES
COOKING TIME: 17 MINUTES
PER SERVING (4): KCAL: 537; FAT: 33.1G; CARBS: 37.28G; PROTEIN: 21.46G; SUGARS: 4.84G; FIBRE: 0.3G

INGRENKEDIENTS:

- 250 ml milk
- 125 ml vegetable oil
- 300 g tapioca flour
- 2 eggs, cracked into a bowl
- 70 g finely grated cheddar cheese

INSTRUCTIONS:

Step 1: Preheat the air fryer to 180°C.

Step 2: Heat the milk and oil in a saucepan over low heat (on a stovetop) but don't let it boil. Whisk in the tapioca flour until combined. Transfer the dough to the bowl of a stand mixer and knead for 2 minutes or until smooth and partially cooled.

Step 3: Add the eggs one after the other and beat after each addition until smooth. Add the cheese and beat until well combined.

Step 4: Damp your hands with water and shape balls (15 g in size) from the mixture.

Step 5: Line the air fryer basket with parchment paper and use a small knife to create a few holes through the paper.

Step 6: Place the dough balls in the air fryer with some spacing but not overlapping each other and bake for 15 minutes or until the puffs are golden brown and risen. You can bake the balls in batches based on the size of your cooking unit.

Step 7: Transfer the bread puffs to a wire rack to cool completely.

6. CHOCOLATE CHIP COOKIE PUFFS

Chocolate chip cookies are classics for breakfast, snack time, and dessert. Here, I add a little character, making them like mini bread puffs. They are soft, chewy, and so filling.

PREPARATION TIME: 10 MINUTES
COOKING TIME: 9 MINUTES
PER SERVING (4): KCAL: 818; FAT: 48.93G; CARBS: 83.99G; PROTEIN: 10.73G; SUGARS: 39.73G; FIBRE: 7.3G

INGREDIENTS:

- 110 g unsalted butter, melted
- 60 g granulated sugar
- 60 g dark brown sugar
- 1 tsp. vanilla extract
- 1 large egg, cracked into a bowl
- 300 g plain flour
- 1 tsp. baking soda
- 1 tsp. kosher salt
- 225 g bittersweet chocolate chips, 70% to 85%

INSTRUCTIONS:

Step 1: Preheat the air fryer to 160°C.

Step 2: In a bowl, whisk the butter, both sugars, vanilla, and egg until smooth. Sift in the flour, baking soda, and salt. Mix the ingredients until smooth batter forms. Add the chocolate chips and fold it in well.

Step 3: Line the air fryer basket with parchment paper and use a small knife to create a few holes through the paper.

Step 4: Add 2 tbsp. of the dough to your hands and roll it into a ball. Make more balls the same way with the remaining dough.

Step 5: Add the dough balls into the air fryer basket with spaces in between, about 4 to 7 pieces or as many as your air fryer can take. You may need to work in batches.

Step 6: Bake for 7 to 9 minutes or until the cookies are golden brown and slightly puffed up.

Step 7: Remove the cookie puffs onto a wire rack to cool.

Step 8: Serve them warm.

7. COFFEE MUG CAKE

This coffee cake is straightforward to make and elevates your coffee love even better.

PREPARATION TIME: 5 MINUTES
COOKING TIME: 8 MINUTES
PER SERVING (1): KCAL: 85; FAT: 4.13G; CARBS: 9.71G; PROTEIN: 2.22G; SUGARS: 4.82G; FIBRE: 0.2G

INGRENKEDIENTS:

- 1 large egg
- 1 tbsp. unsalted butter, melted
- 45 g plain flour
- 1/2 tsp. espresso powder
- 1/2 tsp. baking powder
- 2½ tsp. granulated sugar
- ½ tsp. vanilla extract

INSTRUCTIONS:

Step 1: Preheat the air fryer to 175°C.

Step 2: Crack the egg into a mug and whisk with the butter. Add the flour, espresso powder, baking powder, and sugar. Whisk until smooth and mix the vanilla in.

Step 3: Sit the mug in the air fryer and bake for 5 to 8 minutes or until the cake sets when you test it with a toothpick.

Step 4: Take out the mug and let it cool for about 5 minutes.

Step 5: Serve the mug cake with an extra cup of coffee, however you like it.

8. COTTAGE CHEESE PANCAKES

This pancake is meant to be one large fluffy one, so the entire family can enjoy slices with other breakfast options. It is rich with vanilla, brown sugar, and cinnamon and can very well be made into smaller sizes with smaller pans.

PREPARATION TIME: 10 MINUTES
COOKING TIME: 10 MINUTES
PER SERVING (4): KCAL: 200; FAT: 6.93G; CARBS: 18.05G; PROTEIN: 15.16G; SUGARS: 4.89G; FIBRE: 0.6G

INGREDIENTS:

- 3 eggs
- 340 g cottage cheese
- 1 tsp. vanilla extract
- 115 g plain flour
- 1/2 tsp. baking powder
- 1 tbsp. brown sugar
- 1/2 tsp. ground cinnamon

INSTRUCTIONS:

Step 1: Preheat the air fryer to 175°C.

Step 2: Crack the eggs into a bowl and whisk them with the cottage cheese and vanilla until smooth. Add the flour, baking powder, brown sugar, and cinnamon. Whisk until smooth batter forms.

Step 3: Grease a 20-cm-diameter round pan with cooking spray and pour in the batter. Hit it a few times on a surface to spread the batter out evenly. You can use a smaller pan for this if you only need to make the pancake in smaller batches.

Step 4: Put the pan in the air fryer and bake for 10 minutes or until the pancake rises and sets within when checked with a toothpick.

Step 5: Remove the pan and let the pancake cool in it for a few minutes. Transfer the pancake to a plate.

Step 6: Slice and enjoy the pancake as it is or dress it with your favourite toppings. Some options to consider are soured cream, fresh fruits, maple syrup, and cinnamon.

9. COTTAGE CHEESE AND SWEET PEPPER MUFFINS

If you're like me who loves some savouriness for breakfast, these muffins will do you lots of good. They pack much flavour from the sweet peppers and double cheesiness, but with some healthy notes too.

PREPARATION TIME: 15 MINUTES
COOKING TIME: 30 MINUTES
PER SERVING (4): KCAL: 316; FAT: 19.91G; CARBS: 16.37G; PROTEIN: 19.21G; SUGARS: 3.88G; FIBRE: 2.3G

INGRENKEDIENTS:

- 40 g corn flour
- 120 g almond flour
- A pinch of garlic powder
- 1 tsp. baking powder
- A pinch of kosher salt
- 5 large eggs, crack into a bowl
- 170 g cottage cheese
- 60 ml almond milk
- 105 g finely chopped sweet peppers, any colour of choice
- 45 g finely chopped fresh chives
- 115 g crumbled feta cheese

INSTRUCTIONS:

Step 1: Preheat the air fryer to 190°C.

Step 2: In a bowl, mix the corn flour, almond flour, garlic powder, baking powder, and salt. In another bowl, whisk the eggs, cottage cheese, and almond milk. Combine both mixtures until smooth batter forms and fold in the sweet peppers, chives, and feta cheese.

Step 3: Grease a four-cup muffin tin with cooking spray and pour in the batter two-thirds way up each tin. You would need to do this in batches to make 8 muffins.

Step 4: Place the muffin tin in the air fryer and bake for 30 minutes or until a toothpick inserted into each muffin comes out clean.

Step 5: Remove the tin from the air fryer and let the muffins cool in it for 10 minutes. Transfer them to a wire rack and let them cool completely.

Step 6: Serve the muffins.

10. CREAMY SCRAMBLED EGGS

A good breakfast set should have some eggs of sorts and scrambled eggs happen to be a favourite. To make it extra special, whisk in some double cream instead of milk and enjoy all that yumminess.

PREPARATION TIME: 10 MINUTES
COOKING TIME: 10 MINUTES
PER SERVING (4): KCAL: 131; FAT: 10.81G; CARBS: 0.85G; PROTEIN: 7.45G; SUGARS: 0.41G; FIBRE: 0.1G

INGREDIENTS:

- 7.5 g unsalted butter
- 4 eggs
- 2 tbsp. double cream
- Salt and black pepper to taste
- 60 g grated cheddar cheese
- Chopped fresh chives for garnish

INSTRUCTIONS:

Step 1: Preheat the air fryer to 150°C and add the butter to an air fryer safe-pan. Let the butter melt for 2 minutes.

Step 2: Crack the eggs into a bowl and whisk them along with the double cream, salt, and black pepper. Now, mix in the cheddar cheese.

Step 3: Pour the egg mixture into the pan with the butter and cook for 10 minutes while stirring the eggs every 2 minutes or until they are set to your desire.

Step 4: Remove the pan and spoon the eggs onto serving plates. Garnish with some chives and serve warm.

The UK Air Fryer Cookbook for Beginners

11. EGGS AND SAUSAGE CASSEROLE

You can say this casserole is just an elevated way to enjoy omelette. It is rich with sausages and the cream and cheese factor makes it quite irresistible.

PREPARATION TIME: 15 MINUTES
COOKING TIME: 25 MINUTES
PER SERVING (4): KCAL: 252; FAT: 19.53G; CARBS: 4G; PROTEIN: 14.47G; SUGARS: 1.64G; FIBRE: 0.7G

INGREDIENTS:

- 1 small onion, diced
- ½ green bell pepper, diced
- 3 pork breakfast sausages, sliced into bite-size pieces
- 6 eggs
- 60 ml double cream
- Salt and black pepper to taste
- 1/2 tsp. garlic powder
- 60 g grated mozzarella

INSTRUCTIONS:

Step 1: Preheat the air fryer to 180°C.

Step 2: In a baking dish with a good size for your air fryer, spread the onion, bell pepper, and sausages.

Step 3: Crack the eggs into a bowl and whisk with the double cream, salt, and black pepper. Pour the egg mixture over the sausage mix in the dish. Then, spread the mozzarella cheese over the eggs.

Step 4: Put the baking dish in the air fryer and bake for 20 to 25 minutes or until the eggs set within. You can test this by inserting a toothpick into the casserole and if it comes out clean, then the eggs are set.

Step 5: Take out the dish, let the casserole cool for a few minutes, and then serve warm.

12. GRANOLA-STUFFED BAKED APPLES

These apples are a cooler way of enjoying a bowl of granola with some fruits. A little twist that yields softer apples with fruitier juices all for your enjoyment.

PREPARATION TIME: 10 MINUTES
COOKING TIME: 20 MINUTES
PER SERVING (4): KCAL: 335; FAT: 14.61G; CARBS: 51.57G; PROTEIN: 3.74G; SUGARS: 33.13G; FIBRE: 6.3G

INGREDIENTS:

- 4 apples, any type of choice
- 225 g granola
- 60 g raisins
- 45 g melted butter, unsalted
- 1 tsp. all-spice seasoning

INSTRUCTIONS:

Step 1: Preheat the air fryer to 175°C.

Step 2: Core the apples with a knife, making sure to create a wide hole enough for stuffing in the granola mix.

Step 3: In a bowl, mix the granola, raisins, butter, and all-spice seasoning. Spoon the mixture into the apples all the way to the top.

Step 4: Carefully sit the apples in the air fryer basket and bake for 20 minutes or until the apples are tender.

Step 5: Remove the apples to a plate, let them cool slightly, and serve them with some yoghurt.

13. HERBED EGG WHITES AND FETA ENGLISH MUFFINS

These aren't your regular breakfast sandwiches. One bite into them and you'd be sold to keep having them repeatedly. They are rich with basil flavours, some chives for extra depth, and rich with egg whites and feta for calming colour and much flavour.

PREPARATION TIME: 10 MINUTES
COOKING TIME: 10 MINUTES
PER SERVING (4): KCAL: 732; FAT: 36G; CARBS: 83.01G; PROTEIN: 26.58G; SUGARS: 18.52G; FIBRE: 13.6G

INGRENKEDIENTS:

- Cooking spray
- 4 large egg whites
- 300 ml double cream
- A pinch of salt or to taste
- 60 g finely chopped fresh basil
- 75 g finely chopped fresh chives
- 60 g basil pesto
- 60 g salted butter, at room temperature
- 170 g crumbled feta cheese
- 12 whole-wheat English muffins, split

INSTRUCTIONS:

Step 1: Preheat the air fryer to 150°C and grease an air fryer safe-pan with cooking spray.

Step 2: In a bowl, whisk the egg whites with the double cream and salt until smooth. Add the chives and basil, and mix well.

Step 3: Pour the egg mixture into the pan and cook in the air fryer for 10 minutes while stirring the eggs every 2 minutes or until they are scrambled and set to your desire.

Step 4: Remove the pan from the air fryer.

Step 5: Spread the butter on the inner sides of the muffins. On the bottom parts of the muffins, spread the pesto and top with the herbed eggs and feta cheese. Cover with the top parts of the muffins.

Step 6: Serve the muffin sandwiches warm.

14. LEMON BLUEBERRY BREAD

Lemon blueberry bread bursts with so much freshness for the morning. It is such a great way to make homemade bread with character.

PREPARATION TIME: 15 MINUTES
COOKING TIME: 25 MINUTES
PER SERVING (4): KCAL: 559; FAT: 26.75G; CARBS: 82.97G; PROTEIN: 9.19G; SUGARS: 44.09G; FIBRE: 0.01G

INGREDIENTS:

- 110 g butter
- 170 g granulated sugar
- 2 eggs
- 120 ml milk
- 340 g plain flour
- 1 tsp. baking powder
- 1 tsp. salt
- 2 tbsp. fresh lemon juice
- 1 tbsp. fresh lemon zest
- 285 g fresh blueberries

INSTRUCTIONS:

Step 1: Preheat the air fryer to 160°C.

Step 2: In a large bowl, using a hand mixer (or stand mixer if you have one), cream the butter and sugar until smooth. Add the eggs and whisk until smooth. Add the milk and whisk again until smooth.

Step 3: Sift the flour, baking powder, and salt into the egg mixture and whisk until smooth batter forms.

Step 4: Stir in the lemon juice and fold in the blueberries.

Step 5: Grease a loaf pan (safe for your air fryer) with butter and pour the bread batter into it. Use a spoon to level the top evenly.

Step 6: Place the pan in the air fryer and bake for 20 to 25 minutes or until a toothpick inserted into the bread pulls out clean.

Step 7: Remove the pan from the air fryer and let the bread cool in it for 10 minutes. After, transfer the bread to a wire rack and let it cool completely.

Step 8: Slice the bread and enjoy it with your morning cup of tea, coffee, or juice. Spread on some butter for even better flavour.

15. LEMON POPPY SEED MUFFINS

The zing is right with these muffins and they burst open with so much freshness. Breaking the muffins into several dots of poppy seeds is intriguing and will whet your appetite.

PREPARATION TIME: 10 MINUTES
COOKING TIME: 12 MINUTES
PER SERVING (4): KCAL: 357; FAT: 21.48G; CARBS: 27.57G; PROTEIN: 12.72G; SUGARS: 1.02G; FIBRE: 1.3G

INGRENKEDIENTS:

- 225 g plain flour
- 1 tsp. baking powder
- ½ tsp. baking soda
- A pinch of salt
- 75 g sugar
- 1 tbsp. fresh lemon zest
- 1 tbsp. fresh lemon juice
- 80 ml soured cream
- 1 egg, cracked into a bowl
- 1 tsp. vanilla extract
- 60 ml melted butter
- 1 tbsp. poppy seeds
- Cooking spray

INSTRUCTIONS:

Step 1: Preheat the air fryer to 160°C.

Step 2: In a bowl, mix the flour, baking powder, baking soda, salt, sugar, and lemon zest. In another bowl, whisk the soured cream, lemon juice, egg, vanilla, and butter. Combine both mixtures until smooth batter forms. Add the poppy seeds and mix in well.

Step 3: Grease a four-cup muffin tin with cooking spray and pour in the batter two-thirds way up each tin.

Step 4: Place the muffin tin in the air fryer and bake for 12 minutes or until a toothpick inserted into each muffin comes out clean.

Step 5: Remove the tin from the air fryer and let the muffins cool in it for 10 minutes. Transfer them to a wire rack and let them cool completely.

Step 6: Serve the muffins.

16. MAPLE BACON

You could throw some bacon into the air fryer as a quick way to get some breakfast on the table. But how about coating them with maple syrup for an extra touch of sweetness and flavour?

PREPARATION TIME: 5 MINUTES
COOKING TIME: 10 MINUTES
PER SERVING (4): KCAL: 513; FAT: 44.54G; CARBS: 14.15G; PROTEIN: 14.22G; SUGARS: 12.85G; FIBRE: 0G

INGREDIENTS:

- 450 g sliced bacon
- 120 ml maple syrup

INSTRUCTIONS:

Step 1: Preheat the air fryer to 200°C.

Step 2: Lay the bacon on a wide plate and brush them on both sides with the maple syrup.

Step 3: Lay the bacon in the air fryer basket without overlapping and cook them for 8 to 10 minutes or until they are golden brown and crispy.

Step 4: Remove the bacon onto a plate to cool for a few minutes and then serve them.

17. PERFECTLY BOILED EGGS

Perfect in this case would be up to you. As a beginner user, making boiled eggs in the air fryer is your first pass to success. Whether you like them soft or hard, this recipe will be perfect for you.

PREPARATION TIME: 5 MINUTES
COOKING TIME: 13 TO 17 MINUTES
PER SERVING (4): KCAL: 374; FAT: 23.11G; CARBS: 1.75G; PROTEIN: 30.52G; SUGARS: 0.9G; FIBRE: 0G

INGRENKEDIENTS:

- 4 eggs

INSTRUCTIONS:

Step 1: Preheat the air fryer to 120°C.

Step 2: Place the eggs in the basket and close the air fryer.

Step 3: Cook the eggs for 13 to 17 minutes for soft-boiled to hard-boiled eggs, respectively.

Step 4: When they are ready, use tongs to lift them into an ice water bath. Let them sit for 5 minutes before peeling them.

Step 5: Enjoy the eggs with your other breakfast options.

18. MINI QUICHE WITH BACON AND CHIVES

A little crunch for breakfast is great and these mini quiches are worthy of all that goodness. They pack little bacon pieces and some chives that bring freshness to each bite. Just filling and delicious for the morning!

PREPARATION TIME: 10 MINUTES
COOKING TIME: 40 MINUTES
PER SERVING(4): KCAL: 647; FAT: 48.56G; CARBS: 33G; PROTEIN: 20.39; SUGARS: 2.17G; FIBRE: 2.1G

INGREDIENTS:

- 4 slices bacon
- 5 eggs
- 120 ml double cream
- A pinch of cayenne pepper
- A pinch of sweet paprika
- 2 tsp. yellow mustard
- Salt and black pepper to taste
- 150 g chopped fresh chives
- 85 g grated Gruyere cheese
- 1 (410 g) package refrigerated shortcrust pastry
- Cooking spray

INSTRUCTIONS:

Step 1: Preheat the air fryer to 200°C.

Step 2: Lay the bacon in the air fryer basket without overlapping and cook them for 8 to 10 minutes or until they are golden brown and crispy. Remove the bacon onto a plate, let them cook, and chop them to your desired sizes.

Step 3: Crack the eggs into a bowl and whisk them with the double cream, cayenne pepper (if using), paprika, mustard, salt, and black pepper. Add the chives and Gruyere cheese, and fold in well.

Step 4: Roll out the pastry and using an 8-cm round cookie cutter, cut 4 rounds from the pastry.

Step 5: Grease a four-cup muffin tin with cooking spray and line the cups with the cut out pastry while crimping the edges.

Step 6: Fill the dough cups with the egg mixture and place the muffin tin in the air fryer. Bake for 30 minutes or until the eggs are set.

Step 7: Take out the muffin tin and let the tin cool slightly. Remove the quiches and serve warm.

19. RASPBERRY AND WHITE CHOCOLATE SCONES

What a colourful start to the day with these chocolate-rich scones. Even better, they burst with such soothing fruity flavours that is an enriching kick for the morning.

PREPARATION TIME: 10 MINUTES
COOKING TIME: 14 MINUTES
PER SERVING (4): KCAL: 464; FAT: 16.89G; CARBS: 66.77G; PROTEIN: 10.35G; SUGARS: 6.9G; FIBRE: 4.6G

INGREDIENTS:

- 300 g self-raising flour, plus extra for dusting
- 40 g cold butter, chopped
- 60 g white chocolate, chopped
- 185 ml milk, plus 1 tbsp. extra for brushing
- 60 g frozen raspberries
- Icing sugar for dusting

INSTRUCTIONS:

Step 1: Preheat the air fryer to 180°C.

Step 2: Add the flour and butter to a bowl and use your hands to mix them until the mixture resembles fine breadcrumbs. Stir in the white chocolate and make a dough at the centre.

Step 3: Pour the milk into the created hole and use a flat-blade knife to mix until mostly combined. Add the raspberries and gently fold in.

Step 4: Dust a surface with some flour and turn the dough onto it. Gently knead the dough until just smooth and press it into a 2-cm-thick disc.

Step 5: Using a 5-cm round pastry cutter, cut out 12 pieces from the dough, working as close as possible.

Step 6: Line the air fryer basket with parchment paper and use a small knife to cut small holes on the paper to aid air circulation.

Step 7: Arrange the dough pieces in the air fryer and brush their tops with a little milk. Bake the scones for 12 to 14 minutes or until they are golden brown and risen.

Step 8: Remove the scones onto a wire rack to cool. Dust them with some icing sugar and serve.

20. RASPBERRY TOASTIE CUPS

The colour these toastie cups give is amazing! It whets your appetite in a moment and enriches you for a good day start.

PREPARATION TIME: 1 HOUR 10 MINUTES
COOKING TIME: 15 MINUTES
PER SERVING (4): KCAL: 393; FAT: 15.31G; CARBS: 48.28G; PROTEIN: 17.86G; SUGARS: 22.57G; FIBRE: 10.7G

INGREDIENTS:

For the toastie cups:

- Cooking spray
- 4 slices Italian bread, cut into 1.5 cm cubes
- 225 g fresh or frozen raspberries
- 110 g soft cheese, cut into 1.5 cm cubes
- 4 large eggs
- 2 tbsp. maple syrup
- 240 ml whole milk

For the raspberry syrup:

- 160 ml water
- 4 tsp. corn flour
- 910 g fresh or frozen raspberries
- 2 tbsp. maple syrup
- 2 tbsp. lemon juice
- 1 tsp. grated lemon zest
- A pinch of ground cinnamon (optional)

INSTRUCTIONS:

For the toastie cups:

Step 1: Lightly grease four medium ramekins with cooking spray and equally divide half of the bread into them. Also, share the raspberries and soft cheese on them. Then, share the remaining bread on them.

Step 2: Crack the eggs into a bowl and whisk them with the maple syrup and milk. Pour the eggs over the content in the ramekins. Cover the ramekins with foil and refrigerate them for 1 hour.

Step 3: Preheat the air fryer to 160°C.

Step 4: After an hour, remove the ramekins from the fridge and uncover them. Place them in the air fryer and bake for 12 to 15 minutes or until the eggs set or the bread isn't soggy.

For the raspberry syrup:

Step 5: In a saucepan, mix the water and corn flour until smooth.

Step 6: Add three cups of the raspberries, maple syrup, lemon juice, and lemon zest. Mix and cook over medium heat (on a stovetop) for 2 minutes or until the raspberries break and the sauce thickens. Strain the syrup and discard the seeds.

Step 7: Stir the remaining raspberries into the syrup and it is ready for serving.

Step 8: Remove the ramekins from the air fryer, sprinkle them with some cinnamon if you like, and drizzle some raspberry syrup on them.

21. ROASTED ORANGES WITH YOGHURT

Technically, these roasted oranges are great late-night snacks but they taste so good that they become an irresistible breakfast option. Pair them with yoghurt and you have a healthy breakfast that is summery and a breeze.

PREPARATION TIME: 5 MINUTES
COOKING TIME: 5 MINUTES
PER SERVING (4): KCAL: 49; FAT: 0.14G; CARBS: 12.62G; PROTEIN: 0.61G; SUGARS: 9.46G; FIBRE: 2G

INGRENKEDIENTS:

- 1 navel orange, peeled and sliced
- 1 blood orange, peeled and sliced
- 1 tbsp. maple syrup
- 1 tsp. ground cinnamon or to taste
- Yoghurt for serving

INSTRUCTIONS:

Step 1: Preheat the air fryer to 200°C.

Step 2: In a bowl, toss the oranges with the maple syrup and cinnamon.

Step 3: Put the oranges in the air fryer basket and roast for 4 to 5 minutes or until they are slightly caramelised.

Step 4: Take the oranges out and serve them with some yoghurt. And more cinnamon if you like.

22. SUN-DRIED TOMATO AND ROCKET EGG MUFFINS

These are colourful treats that will draw your attention from a distance. They smell great and taste just as awesome.

PREPARATION TIME: 10 MINUTES
COOKING TIME: 10 MINUTES
PER SERVING (4): KCAL: 170; FAT: 11.77G; CARBS: 3.91G; PROTEIN: 11.92G; SUGARS: 1.79G; FIBRE: 0.6G

INGREDIENTS:

- 6 large eggs
- 2 tbsp. double cream
- Salt and black pepper to taste
- 60 g grated Parmesan cheese
- 60 g chopped sun-dried tomatoes
- 60 g baby rocket

INSTRUCTIONS:

Step 1: Preheat the air fryer to 170°C and grease a four-cup muffin tin with cooking spray.

Step 2: Crack the eggs into a bowl and whisk with the double cream, salt, and black pepper. Add the Parmesan cheese, sun-dried tomatoes, and rocket. Divide the egg mixture into the holes of the muffin tin.

Step 3: Place the tin in the air fryer and bake for 8 to 10 minutes or until the eggs set within when checked with a toothpick.

Step 4: Take out the tin, let it cool for a minute, and remove the egg cups.

Step 5: Serve the egg cups warm.

23. SWEET POTATO HASH

There are many styles of making sweet potato hash. Some people like them grated, others diced, and some like them cooked like muffins. I particularly like them cubed because they create a more filling look. But, for this recipe, you can grate the potatoes and they should turn out great and crispier.

PREPARATION TIME: 15 MINUTES
COOKING TIME: 25 MINUTES
PER SERVING (4): KCAL: 324; FAT: 24.8G; CARBS: 23.97G; PROTEIN: 2.18G; SUGARS: 7.8G; FIBRE: 3.9G

INGRENKEDIENTS:

- 3 medium sweet potatoes, peeled and cut into 2 cm cubes or grated
- 110 g diced white onion (or grated)
- 110 g chopped green sweet peppers
- 2 garlic cloves, minced
- 75 g diced celery
- 1 tbsp. olive oil
- 1/2 tsp. paprika
- 1 tsp. Cajun seasoning
- Salt and black pepper to taste
- 3 cooked bacon slices, crumbled
- 1/2 tsp. dried chives

INSTRUCTIONS:

Step 1: Preheat the air fryer to 200°C.

Step 2: In a bowl, add the sweet potatoes, onion, green sweet peppers, garlic, celery, olive oil, paprika, Cajun seasoning, salt, and black pepper.

Step 3: Pour the sweet potato mixture into the air fryer basket and cook for 20 to 25 minutes or until they are golden brown and fork tender.

Step 4: Pour them into a bowl and add the bacon and chives. Toss them well and, at this point, you can add some hot sauce if you wish to.

Step 5: Enjoy them warm with some eggs.

24. THREE CHEESE EGG CUPS

An extra cheesy morning wouldn't be bad, would it? Throw your favourite cheeses into some egg cups and have yourself a yummy treat.

PREPARATION TIME: 7 MINUTES
COOKING TIME: 10 MINUTES
PER SERVING (4): KCAL: 217; FAT: 16.24G; CARBS: 2.1G; PROTEIN: 15.12G; SUGARS: 0.54G; FIBRE: 0.1G

INGREDIENTS:

- 6 large eggs
- 2 tbsp. double cream
- Salt and black pepper to taste
- 60 g grated cheddar cheese
- 60 g grated Parmesan cheese
- 60 g grated Gruyere cheese

INSTRUCTIONS:

Step 1: Preheat the air fryer to 170°C and grease a four-cup muffin tin with cooking spray.

Step 2: Crack the eggs into a bowl and whisk with the double cream, salt, and black pepper. Add the cheeses and mix well. Divide the egg mixture into the holes of the muffin tin.

Step 3: Place the tin in the air fryer and bake for 8 to 10 minutes or until the eggs set within and the cheeses have melted.

Step 4: Take out the tin, let it cool for a minute, and remove the egg cups.

Step 5: Serve the egg cups warm.

25. VEGGIE FRITTATA

There are no rules when it comes to making a veggie frittata. Add or subtract as many vegetables as you like and choose any ones that catch your fancy.

PREPARATION TIME: 10 MINUTES
COOKING TIME: 25 MINUTES
PER SERVING (4): KCAL: 224; FAT: 14.28G; CARBS: 9.23G; PROTEIN: 14.5G; SUGARS: 0.99G; FIBRE: 1G

INGRENKEDIENTS:

- 4 eggs
- 1 tsp. mustard powder
- A pinch of salt
- 225 g diced pre-cooked potato
- 225 g grated cheese
- 60 g chopped onion
- 110 g baby spinach leaves, roughly chopped

INSTRUCTIONS:

Step 1: Preheat the air fryer to 160°C.

Step 2: Crack the eggs into a bowl and whisk them with the mustard powder and salt. Add the potato, cheese, onion, and spinach.

Step 3: Grease an 8-cm-diameter round pan with cooking spray and pour the egg mixture in it.

Step 4: Place the pan in the air fryer and bake for 20 to 25 minutes or until the eggs are set all around and the top is golden brown on top.

Step 5: Remove the pan and let the frittata rest for 2 to 3 minutes.

Step 6. Transfer the frittata onto a serving platter and slice.

Step 7: Serve.

SECTION 2.

SNACKS

**Don't Forget To Get The Color Images FREE!
Simply Scan The QR Code Below!**

Please scan the QR code below to access your bonus PDF with all 150 recipes with full coloured photos & beautiful designs alongside!

This is the only way we can get the recipes with coloured photos to you & keep the book as reasonably priced as possible.

Also, once downloaded you can take the PDF with you digitally wherever you go- meaning you can cook these recipes wherever you may be! (As long as you have an air fryer!)

We hope you enjoy and do let us know your feedback!

(INSERT QR CODE HERE)

STEP BY STEP Guide-

1. Open Your Phones (Or Any Device You Want The Book On) Back Camera. The Back Camera Is The One You use as if you are taking a picture of someone.
2. Simply point your Camera at the QR code and 'tap' the QR code with your finger to focus the camera.
3. A link / pop up will appear. Simply tap that (and make sure you have internet connection) and the FREE PDF containing all of the coloured images should appear.
4. Now you have access to these FOREVER. Simply 'Bookmark' The tab it opened on, or download the document and take wherever you want.
5. Repeat this on any device you want it on! (If you want it on a laptop, simply email the document to yourself!)

Any issues please email us at **vicandersonpublishing@gmail.com** and we will be happy to help!!

1. APPLE HAND PIES

One hearty snack for a lunch pack or picnic basket would be apple hand pies. What's your Sunday looking like? You might want to schedule these hand pies in.

PREPARATION TIME: 10 MINUTES
COOKING TIME: 10 MINUTES
PER SERVING (4): KCAL: 677; FAT: 30.41G; CARBS: 96.95G; PROTEIN: 5.05G; SUGARS: 29.11G; FIBRE: 2.8G

INGRENKEDIENTS:

- 2 (400 g) refrigerated package pie crusts, defrosted
- ½ (590) apple pie filling
- 1 large egg
- Water
- 1 tbsp. raw brown sugar

INSTRUCTIONS:

Step 1: Preheat the air fryer to 175°C.

Step 2: Lay out the pie crusts on a clean flat surface and cut out four 12-cm-diameter circles.

Step 3: Share the apple filling on one half of each of the circles and fold the empty half over the filling. Using a fork, crimp the edges to seal the pie.

Step 4: Crack the egg into a bowl and beat with the water. Brush the tops of the pie with the egg and sprinkle the sugar on top.

Step 5: Mist the air fryer basket with cooking spray and place two pies in it.

Step 6: Bake for 10 minutes or until the crust is golden brown and the apple filling is bubbly.

Step 7: Remove the hand pies onto a wire rack to cool while you bake the others.

Step 8: Serve them warm or cold.

2. BANANA AND ALMOND MUFFINS

I'm not sure where to place these muffins between breakfast and snack. But I guess because they are richly textured, they'll be a fantastic quick fill through the day.

PREPARATION TIME: 10 MINUTES
COOKING TIME: 30 MINUTES
PER SERVING (4): KCAL: 448; FAT: 19.75G; CARBS: 62.12G; PROTEIN: 7.89G; SUGARS: 32.7G; FIBRE: 2.8G

INGREDIENTS:

For the dry ingredients:

- 225 g plain flour
- 1/2 tsp. ground cinnamon
- 1/2 tsp. baking powder
- 1/2 tsp. baking soda
- A pinch of salt

For the wet ingredients:

- 1 very large banana, peeled and mashed
- 120 ml plain yoghurt
- 60 ml vegetable oil
- 110 g packed brown sugar
- 1 large egg, cracked into a bowl

For folding in:

- 60 g chopped almonds

INSTRUCTIONS:

Step 1: Preheat the air fryer to 190°C.

Step 2: Add the dry ingredients to a bowl and mix well. Do the same thing for the wet ingredients in another bowl and combine both mixtures until you achieve a smooth batter. Add the chopped almonds and fold them in.

Step 3: Grease a four-cup muffin tin with cooking spray and pour in the batter two-thirds way up each tin. You would need to do this twice to make 8 muffins.

Step 4: Place the muffin tin in the air fryer and bake for 15 to 20 minutes or until a toothpick inserted into each muffin comes out clean.

Step 5: Remove the tin from the air fryer and let the muffins cool in it for 10 minutes. Remove them onto a wire rack and let them cool completely. Bake the remaining batter the same way.

Step 6: Serve the muffins.

The UK Air Fryer Cookbook for Beginners

3. BLUEBERRY OAT TRAYBAKE

I like versatility when using ingredients and this tray bake is just a fine deconstruction of an oatmeal bowl. It is well geared for a nourishing snack.

PREPARATION TIME: 10 MINUTES
COOKING TIME: 45 MINUTES
PER SERVING (4): KCAL: 716; FAT: 27.94 G; CARBS: 100.02G; PROTEIN: 22.25G; SUGARS: 40.92G; FIBRE: 12.9G

INGREDIENTS:

- 450 g old-fashioned oats
- 150 g roughly chopped pecans
- 1 tsp. baking powder
- 2 tsp. ground cinnamon
- A pinch of ground nutmeg
- 1 tsp. salt
- 2 large eggs, cracked into a bowl
- 420 ml milk of choice
- 80 ml honey
- 2 tbsp. melted unsalted butter
- 2 tsp. vanilla extract
- 560 g fresh blueberries
- 2 tsp. raw brown sugar

INSTRUCTIONS:

Step 1: Preheat the air fryer to 190°C and set aside a baking dish that can fit into your air fryer.

Step 2: In a bowl, mix the oats, pecans, baking powder, cinnamon, nutmeg, and salt. In another bowl, whisk the eggs, milk, honey, butter, and vanilla until smooth. Combine both mixtures and mix them smoothly. Fold in half of the blueberries and pour the mixture into the baking dish. Wiggle the dish a little to spread the batter evenly. After, spread the remaining blueberries on top and sprinkle with the sugar.

Step 3: Put the dish in the air fryer and bake for 40 to 45 minutes or until set within when checked with a toothpick.

Step 4: Remove the dish and let it cool.

Step 5: Cut the oat bake into squares and enjoy.

4. CANDIED LEMON

If you're one of those that enjoys biting into the rinds of lemon, then I present you with a better option. Sugar crisps them up and creates a lovely sweet crunch that you'll enjoy.

PREPARATION TIME: 10 MINUTES
COOKING TIME: 8 HOURS
PER SERVING (4): KCAL: 113; FAT: 0.09G; CARBS: 29.68G; PROTEIN: 0.35G; SUGARS: 27.41G; FIBRE: 0.8G

INGREDIENTS:

- 2 lemons, very thinly sliced
- 110 g granulated or brown sugar

INSTRUCTIONS:

Step 1: Preheat the air fryer to 57°C.

Step 2: Rub the lemon slices on both sides with sugar.

Step 3: Line the air fryer basket with parchment paper and lay the lemon slices in it in a single layer. You may need to work in batches if your air fryer space is small. You may also sprinkle the tops of the lemon with more sugar as desired.

Step 4: Dehydrate the lemons for 8 hours, while turning them after 4 hours of cooking. When the lemons are dry and crispy, they are ready.

Step 5: Remove them onto a serving platter to cool and enjoy them after.

5. CHEESY COURGETTES

Simply slice up some courgettes, throw on some cheese, and you have yourself a lazy delicious snack.

PREPARATION TIME: 15 MINUTES
COOKING TIME: 10 MINUTES
PER SERVING (4): KCAL: 61; FAT: 5.16G; CARBS: 1.78G; PROTEIN: 2.14G; SUGARS: 0.02G; FIBRE: 0.2G

INGRENKEDIENTS:

- 2 large courgettes
- 1 tbsp. olive oil
- 1 tsp. garlic powder
- Salt and black pepper to taste
- 60 g Parmesan cheese

INSTRUCTIONS:

Step 1: Preheat the air fryer to 200°C.

Step 2: Cut the courgettes into 0.5-cm slices and add them to a bowl. You can also cut them into your preferred shapes. Drizzle with olive oil and season with the garlic powder, salt, and black pepper. Toss until well coated.

Step 3: Line the air fryer with parchment paper and arrange the courgettes on it. Sprinkle half of the Parmesan cheese. You may need to do this in batches.

Step 4: Bake for 5 minutes and turn the courgettes over. Sprinkle the remaining cheese on top and bake for 5 more minutes or until the cheese melts and is golden brown.

Step 5: Move the cheesy courgettes onto a plate and serve warm.

6. CHOCOLATE CRUMPETS

Crumpets as chocolate? I know it sounds unusual but don't beat it yet. Give them a shot and be sold.

PREPARATION TIME: 70 TO 100 MINUTES
COOKING TIME: 12 MINUTES
PER SERVING (4+): KCAL: 292; FAT: 10.96G; CARBS: 41.63G; PROTEIN: 8.3G; SUGARS: 7.95G; FIBRE: 2.7G

INGREDIENTS:

- 350 ml milk
- 1 tsp. instant yeast
- 1 tbsp. golden caster sugar
- 45 g cocoa powder
- 165 g plain flour
- 2 tbsp. vegetable oil for greasing

NSTRUCTIONS:

Step 1: Heat 300 ml of the milk in a pot over low heat until bubbles start forming around the edges. Turn the heat off and stir in the yeast, sugar, cocoa powder, and flour until smooth. Cover the pot with a napkin and let the dough rise for 60 to 90 minutes or until doubled and very bubbly.

Step 2: Remove the napkin and mix in the remaining milk, the dough would reduce in size.

Step 3: Preheat the air fryer to 180°C.

Step 4: Brush 4 (9 cm) crumpet rings with vegetable oil and spoon the batter into the rings halfway through.

Step 5: Place the rings in the air fryer and bake for 10 to 12 minutes or until they have risen, are golden brown, and set within.

Step 6: Remove the crumpets onto a wire rack to cool and bake the remaining batter the same way.

Step 7: Enjoy the crumpets as a breakfast side.

7. CHOCOLATE-FILLED DOUGHNUTS

Don't freak out about making doughnut dough. If you can buy them, that'll cut out your prep time by a bunch. Just fill them with chocolate sauce and you have an easy, impressive treat.

PREPARATION TIME: 10 MINUTES
COOKING TIME: 6 MINUTES
PER SERVING (4): KCAL: 778; FAT: 40.77G; CARBS: 96.52G; PROTEIN: 10.45G; SUGARS: 40.28G; FIBRE: 7.3G

INGREDIENTS:

- 1 (400 g) package premade refrigerator dough biscuits
- 250 g dark chocolate bar, broken into pieces
- 45 g butter, melted
- 110 g granulated sugar
- 1 tsp. ground cinnamon

INSTRUCTIONS:

Step 1: Preheat the air fryer to 175°C.

Step 2: Remove the dough from its package and separate the individual biscuits. Use your palm to slightly flatten the biscuit.

Step 3: Place one or two chocolate pieces at the centre of each dough piece and wrap the dough over the chocolate. Freeze the dough balls for 30 minutes.

Step 4: After, mist the air fryer with cooking spray and place the dough balls in it. Bake for 2 to 3 minutes per side or until they are golden brown.

Step 5: Meanwhile, in a bowl, mix the sugar and cinnamon.

Step 6: Remove the doughnut onto a plate, brush the butter on them, and sprinkle with the cinnamon sugar.

Step 7: Serve the doughnuts warm.

8. CINNAMON TORTILLA CHIPS WITH WATERMELON SALSA

These chips are just one of many creative ways to use tortillas. Particularly, they are awesome because of the watermelon pairing that they share. So, refreshing and delicious.

PREPARATION TIME: 15 MINUTES
COOKING TIME: 8 MINUTES
PER SERVING (8): KCAL: 391; FAT: 5.73G; CARBS: 83.11G; PROTEIN: 4.03G; SUGARS: 58.93G; FIBRE: 2.1G

INGREDIENTS:

For the cinnamon chips:

- 8 flour tortillas
- 2 tbsp. melted butter
- 30 g sugar
- 1/2 tsp. ground cinnamon

For the watermelon salsa:

- 225 g finely chopped watermelon, seeds removed
- 1 medium apple, cored and finely chopped
- 2 kiwis, peeled and finely chopped
- 1 tbsp. fresh lemon juice
- 30 g granulated sugar

INSTRUCTIONS:

For the cinnamon chips:

Step 1: Preheat the air fryer to 200°C.

Step 2: Use a knife to cut the tortillas into bite-size triangles, about 8 pieces that can scoop the salsa. Brush them with butter on both sides and put them in a zipper bag.

Step 3: In a small bowl, mix the sugar and cinnamon. Add the cinnamon sugar to the bag, zip it, and shake a few times until the triangles are well-coated with the sugar.

Step 4: Arrange the tortilla triangles in the air fryer in a single layer and bake for 4 minutes or until they are golden brown and crispy.

Step 5: Remove the chips onto a large plate and let them cool.

For the watermelon salsa:

Step 6: In a bowl, combine the watermelon, kiwi, apple, lemon juice, and sugar. Mix well.

Step 7: Serve the cinnamon chips with the watermelon salsa.

9. CRANBERRY MINCE PIES

The tang is right in these pies and the colour of the filling would attract anyone from afar.

PREPARATION TIME: 10 MINUTES
COOKING TIME: 10 MINUTES
PER SERVING (4): KCAL: 556; FAT: 25.66G; CARBS: 76.59G; PROTEIN: 7.24G; SUGARS: 31.29G; FIBRE: 3.4G

INGRENKEDIENTS:

- 2 (400 g) refrigerated package pie crusts, defrosted
- ½ (590 g) cranberry pie filling
- 1 large egg
- Water
- 1 tbsp. granulated sugar

INSTRUCTIONS:

Step 1: Preheat the air fryer to 175°C.

Step 2: Lay out the pie crusts on a clean flat surface and cut out four 12-cm-diameter circles.

Step 3: Divide the filling on one half of each of the circles (not too much to bleed out of the dough) and fold the empty half over the filling. Using a fork, crimp the edges to seal the pie.

Step 4: Crack the egg into a bowl and beat with the water. Brush the tops of the pie with the egg and sprinkle the sugar on top.

Step 5: Mist the air fryer basket with cooking spray and place two pies in it.

Step 6: Bake for 10 minutes or until the crust is golden brown and the cranberry filling is bubbly.

Step 7: Remove the hand pies onto a wire rack to cool while you bake the others.

Step 8: Serve them warm or cold.

10. CRISPY ARTICHOKES

Artichokes are a good snack besides being a nutritious soup vegetable. Sprinkle on some seasoning, whichever that you like and crisp them up. Here, I go with some oregano and lemon zest for zingy, fresh tones.

PREPARATION TIME: 10 MINUTES
COOKING TIME: 14 MINUTES
PER SERVING (4): KCAL: 305; FAT: 4.65G; CARBS: 55.51G; PROTEIN: 14.12G; SUGARS: 3.8G; FIBRE: 18.9G

INGREDIENTS:

- 2 (400 g) cans artichoke hearts in water, drained
- 110 g plain flour
- 2 large eggs
- 225 g panko breadcrumbs
- 1 tsp. dried oregano
- 1 tsp. grated lemon zest
- A pinch of salt

INSTRUCTIONS:

Step 1: Preheat the air fryer to 180°C.

Step 2: Pat dry the artichokes with paper towels and cut them in halves lengthwise. Set them aside.

Step 3: Pour the flour onto a plate, beat the eggs in a bowl, and on another plate, mix the breadcrumbs, oregano, lemon zest, and salt.

Step 4: Dredge the artichoke hearts in the flour, then dip in the eggs, and coat well in the breadcrumb mixture. .

Step 5: Mix the air fryer basket with cooking spray, add the breaded artichoke hearts to it, and mist again with cooking spray.

Step 6: Air fry for 7 minutes per side or until the artichoke hearts are golden brown and crispy.

Step 7: Remove them onto a plate and serve them with your favourite dipping sauce.

11. EXTRA CHEESY TOASTIES

When you can pack up toasties with extra cheese, you should go for it. It's simply a loaded serving of much yumminess. Don't you deserve the treat?

PREPARATION TIME: 10 MINUTES
COOKING TIME: 5 MINUTES
PER SERVING (2): KCAL: 294; FAT: 21.08G; CARBS: 13.04G; PROTEIN: 13.2G; SUGARS: 3.7G; FIBRE: 0.5G

INGREDIENTS:

- 4 slices bread
- 30 g butter, softened
- 4 slices soft melting cheese of choice
- 45 g grated cheddar cheese
- 45 g grated Gruyere cheese

INSTRUCTIONS:

Step 1: Preheat the air fryer to 180°C.

Step 2: Lay out the bread slices and place two soft cheese slices on two pieces. Mix the cheddar and Gruyere cheeses and spread them on the soft cheese. Cover them with the other two bread slices and brush the top and bottom of the bread with butter. It might seem a little messy but that's okay for the perfect crunch.

Step 3: Place the sandwiches in the air fryer and bake for 3 to 5 minutes or until the bread is golden brown and the cheeses have melted.

Step 4: Remove the bread onto a serving platter and slice in halves.

Step 5: Serve them warm.

12. GOLDEN SYRUP FLAPJACKS

They crunch so satisfyingly between your teeth. Make a bunch and pack them up as a carry along snack.

PREPARATION TIME: 10 MINUTES
COOKING TIME: 18 MINUTES
PER SERVING (4): KCAL: 1027; FAT: 57.69G; CARBS: 117.17G; PROTEIN: 17.42G; SUGARS: 50.65G; FIBRE: 10.6G

INGREDIENTS:

- 200 g golden syrup
- 250 g unsalted butter, melted
- 50 g brown sugar
- 400 g porridge oats
- A pinch of salt

INSTRUCTIONS:

Step 1: Preheat the air fryer to 175°C and line a baking tray (with good size for your air fryer) with parchment paper.

Step 2: In a bowl, mix the golden syrup, butter, and brown sugar. Add the oats and salt, and mix well.

Step 3: Spread the mixture on the baking sheet evenly and bake for 15 to 18 minutes or until it is golden brown and dry.

Step 4: Remove the baking sheet from the air fryer and let it cool completely.

Step 5: Cut the snack into thin long bars and enjoy.

13. GRANOLA BARS

You get to extend breakfast to snack time with these bars. And you can use whatever granola that you like.

PREPARATION TIME: 10 MINUTES
COOKING TIME: 18 MINUTES
PER SERVING (4): KCAL: 979; FAT: 65.57G; CARBS: 94.12G; PROTEIN: 8.14G; SUGARS: 63.82G; FIBRE: 4G

INGRENKEDIENTS:

- 200 g honey or maple syrup
- 250 g unsalted butter, melted
- 50 g brown sugar
- 400 g granola, your favourite mix
- A pinch of salt

INSTRUCTIONS:

Step 1: Preheat the air fryer to 175°C and line a baking tray (with good size for your air fryer) with parchment paper.

Step 2: In a bowl, mix the honey or syrup, butter, and brown sugar. Add the granola and salt, and mix well.

Step 3: Spread the mixture on the baking sheet evenly and bake for 15 to 18 minutes or until it is golden brown and dry.

Step 4: Remove the baking sheet from the air fryer and let it cool completely.

Step 5: Cut the snack into bars and enjoy.

14. HAM AND PINEAPPLE MELT

When you have hunger pangs and you're nowhere near lunchtime, fixing up these sweet, savoury, and cheesy muffins will kick up your energy quickly.

PREPARATION TIME: 10 MINUTES
COOKING TIME: 7 MINUTES
PER SERVING (4): KCAL: 169; FAT: 5.38G; CARBS: 21.62G; PROTEIN: 8.85G; SUGARS: 5.54G; FIBRE: 1.9G

INGREDIENTS:

- 2 English muffins, split in half
- 4 slices ham
- 4 pineapples rings
- 60 g grated cheddar cheese

NSTRUCTIONS:

Step 1: Preheat the air fryer to 180°C.

Step 2: On the inner part of each muffin, lay on one ham slice and top each with one pineapple ring and some cheddar cheese.

Step 3: Place the muffins in the air fryer and bake for 4 to 7 minutes or until the cheese melts and the pineapples warm through.

Step 4: Remove the muffin stacks onto a plate and serve warm.

15. HAM, BRIE, AND JAM TOASTIES

These ooze out much inviting colour, flavour, and character. And when you taste them, I can guarantee that you'll make them repeatedly.

PREPARATION TIME: 10 MINUTES
COOKING TIME: 5 MINUTES
PER SERVING (2): KCAL: 293; FAT: 18.93G; CARBS: 17.34G; PROTEIN: 13.54G; SUGARS: 6.12G; FIBRE: 0.7G

INGRENKEDIENTS:

- 2 tbsp. mayonnaise
- 4 bread slices
- 2 tbsp. blueberry jam or jam of choice
- A pinch of black pepper
- 85 g brie cheese, cut into thin slices
- 170 g cooked deli ham, thinly sliced
- 30 g butter

INSTRUCTIONS:

Step 1: Preheat the air fryer to 180°C.

Step 2: Spread the mayonnaise on one side of each bread. Spread the jam on the top of the mayonnaise of two of the bread slices and sprinkle the jam with a bit of black pepper. Lay on the brie cheese and ham, and cover with the mayonnaise side of the other two bread slices. After, spread butter on both outer sides of the bread.

Step 3: Place the sandwiches in the air fryer and bake for 3 to 5 minutes or until the bread is golden brown and the cheese has melted.

Step 4: Remove the bread onto a serving platter and slice in halves.

Step 5: Serve them warm.

16. KALE CHIPS

Just kale and salt but the crunchy bites are delicious and particularly healthy.

PREPARATION TIME: 10 MINUTES
COOKING TIME: 6 MINUTES
PER SERVING (4): KCAL: 58; FAT: 3.9G; CARBS: 4.96G; PROTEIN: 2.43G; SUGARS: 1.28G; FIBRE: 2G

INGREDIENTS:

- 225 g kale
- 1 tbsp. olive oil
- A pinch of salt or to taste

NSTRUCTIONS:

Step 1: Preheat the air fryer to 175°C.

Step 2: Tear the kale leaves off the spine and rinse them well. After, pat them dry with paper towels.

Step 3: Drizzle the olive oil over the kale and season with salt. Use your hands to work the seasoning into the kale.

Step 4: Put the kale into the air fryer basket and air fry for 6 minutes. Make sure to check the kale every 2 minutes to ensure they aren't burning. Once they are crispy, they are ready.

Step 5: Remove the kale onto a plate and spread out to cool completely.

17. MOZZARELLA AND TOMATO HOT POCKETS

These pizza-inspired hot pockets are nothing short of a delicious set. They break open into such ooey-gooey goodness and yet require a handful of ingredients to create.

PREPARATION TIME: 10 MINUTES
COOKING TIME: 20 MINUTES
PER SERVING (4): KCAL: 753; FAT: 50.45G; CARBS: 62.28G; PROTEIN: 3.19G; SUGARS: 7.17G; FIBRE: 2.4G

INGRENKEDIENTS:

- 1 (490 g) box frozen puff pastry, defrosted
- 170 g grated mozzarella cheese
- 1 large tomato, diced
- 1/2 tsp. dried parsley
- Salt and black pepper to taste
- 1 egg beaten
- 1 tbsp. of water

INSTRUCTIONS:

Step 1: Preheat the air fryer to 180°C.

Step 2: Lay out the pastry and cut them into 8 equal squares of 12 x 15 cm size each.

Step 3: Divide the mozzarella cheese onto the centre of each pastry, top with the tomatoes and parsley, and season with a little salt and black pepper. Fold the shorter sides of the pastry over the filling and from one long end, wrap the pastry over the filling. Dip your finger in water, coat the edge of the pastry with it, and seal the pastry. After, brush their tops with the egg wash.

Step 4: Mist the air fryer basket with cooking spray and place the pastries in it. Bake for 15 to 20 minutes or until the pastries are golden brown and the dough cooks.

Step 5: Transfer the hot pockets to a plate, let cool slightly, and enjoy warm.

18. PARMESAN WAFERS

Would you believe that these wafers require only one ingredient—Parmesan cheese? However, you can always create other flavours with other cheeses.

PREPARATION TIME: 5 MINUTES
COOKING TIME: 5 MINUTES
PER SERVING (4): KCAL: 105; FAT: 6.96G; CARBS: 3.48G; PROTEIN: 7.11G; SUGARS: 0.02G; FIBRE: 0G

INGREDIENTS:

- 225 g grated Parmesan cheese

NSTRUCTIONS:

Step 1: Preheat the air fryer to 180°C.

Step 2: Line the air fryer basket with parchment paper.

Step 3: Add 15 g portions of the cheese onto the parchment paper with intervals between them. Bake for 3 to 5 minutes or until the cheese melts, is golden brown, and crispy.

Step 4: Carefully lift off the parchment paper from the air fryer and place the crisps on a rolling pin to cool down.

Step 5: Once cooled, enjoy the crisps.

19. PASTA CHIPS

Throw some cooked pasta into the air fryer to create crunchy snacks that would actually fill you up.

PREPARATION TIME: 15 MINUTES
COOKING TIME: 10 MINUTES
PER SERVING (4): KCAL: 154; FAT: 7.46G; CARBS: 16.62G; PROTEIN: 5.02G; SUGARS: 0.01G; FIBRE: 0.07G

INGRENKEDIENTS:

- 225 g short pasta (ravioli, rigatoni, penne, macaroni, etc.)
- 45 ml olive oil
- 1 tsp. garlic, minced
- 110 g Parmesan cheese, grated
- 1 tsp. salt or to taste
- 1 tsp. black pepper or to taste

INSTRUCTIONS:

Step 1: Cook the pasta according to the package's instructions until al dente (or cooked with a bite to it). Drain the pasta well.

Step 2: Preheat the air fryer to 200°C.

Step 3: In a bowl, combine the pasta and half of the olive oil. Toss well to coat.

Step 4: Spoon the pasta into the air fryer basket and air fry for 8 to 10 minutes or until golden brown and crispy.

Step 5: In a bowl, mix the remaining olive oil, garlic, Parmesan cheese, salt, and black pepper.

Step 6: Remove the pasta onto a bowl, drizzle on the garlic cheese oil, and toss to coat well.

Step 7: Serve the pasta chips.

20. PEANUT BUTTERSCOTCH BARS

I love butterscotch candies so very much. I had to find ways to enjoy them more. Let's just say, these bars are what I'll splurge on, on most days.

PREPARATION TIME: 10 MINUTES
COOKING TIME: 25 MINUTES
PER SERVING (4): KCAL: 1142; FAT: 47.59G; CARBS: 164.99G; PROTEIN: 15.81G; SUGARS: 104.18G; FIBRE: 8.6G

INGREDIENTS:

- 2 large eggs, at room temperature
- 120 ml melted butter
- 225 g brown sugar
- 225 g granulated sugar
- 2 tsp. vanilla extract
- 450 g plain flour
- 2 tsp. baking powder
- A pinch of salt
- ½ cup butterscotch baking chips
- ½ cup peanuts

NSTRUCTIONS:

Step 1: Preheat the air fryer to 175°C and line a baking tray (with good size for your air fryer) with parchment paper.

Step 2: Crack the eggs into a bowl and whisk with the butter, both sugars, and vanilla until smooth. Add the flour, baking powder, and salt. Mix until smooth batter forms and fold in the butterscotch baking chips and peanuts.

Step 3: Spread the batter on the baking sheet evenly and bake for 20 to 25 minutes or until it is set within.

Step 4: Remove the baking sheet from the air fryer and let it cool completely.

Step 5: Cut the snack into bars and enjoy.

21. PEPPERONI CHIPS

I love single-ingredient recipes. How effortless they are. Enjoy pepperoni by simply crisping a few pieces and crunching on them.

PREPARATION TIME: 5 MINUTES
COOKING TIME: 4 MINUTES
PER SERVING (4): KCAL: 350; FAT: 30.83G; CARBS: 0G; PROTEIN: 16.23G; SUGARS: 0G; FIBRE: 0G

INGREDIENTS:

- 225 g pepperoni slices

INSTRUCTIONS:

Step 1: Preheat the air fryer to 200°C.

Step 2: Spread the pepperoni chips in the air fryer basket in a single layer.

Step 3: Bake for 4 minutes or until the pepperoni chips are crispy.

Step 4: Transfer them to a paper towel-lined plate to drain grease.

Step 5: Enjoy them with your preferred dipping sauce.

22. PUMPKIN MUFFINS

In pumpkin season, make good use of the delicious flavour in some muffins. You can also use canned pumpkin all year around.

PREPARATION TIME: 10 MINUTES
COOKING TIME: 25 MINUTES
PER SERVING (4): KCAL: 387; FAT: 15.45G; CARBS: 58.05G; PROTEIN: 5.99G; SUGARS: 28.64G; FIBRE: 4G

INGREDIENTS:

For the dry ingredients:

- 225 g plain flour
- 1/2 tsp. pumpkin pie spice
- 1/2 tsp. baking powder
- 1/2 tsp. baking soda
- A pinch of salt

For the wet ingredients:

- 1 (400 g) can pumpkin puree
- 1 large egg, cracked into a bowl
- 60 ml vegetable oil
- 110 g granulated sugar

INSTRUCTIONS:

Step 1: Preheat the air fryer to 160°C.

Step 2: Add the dry ingredients to a bowl and mix well. Whisk the wet ingredients in another bowl and then combine both mixtures until smooth.

Step 3: Grease a four-cup muffin tin with cooking spray and pour in the batter two-thirds way up each tin. You would need to do this twice to make 8 muffins.

Step 4: Place the muffin tin in the air fryer and bake for 20 to 25 minutes or until a toothpick inserted into each muffin comes out clean.

Step 5: Remove the tin from the air fryer and let the muffins cool in it for 10 minutes. Transfer them onto a wire rack and let them cool completely. Bake the remaining batter the same way.

Step 6: Serve the muffins.

23. SPICED DRIED APPLES

Apple chips are one of my favourite snacks to enjoy. They are crunchy, sweet, and slightly tangy. By sprinkling on some spice, you elevate its aroma.

PREPARATION TIME: 10 MINUTES
COOKING TIME: 15 MINUTES
PER SERVING (4): KCAL: 47; FAT: 0.16G; CARBS: 12.58G; PROTEIN: 0.24G; SUGARS: 9.46G; FIBRE: 2.2G

INGRENKEDIENTS:

- 2 apples, thinly sliced and seeds removed
- A pinch or two of apple pie spice

INSTRUCTIONS:

Step 1: Preheat the air fryer to 150°C.

Step 2: Add the apples and apple pie spice to a large zipper bag and zip the bag. Toss well until they are well-coated with the seasoning.

Step 3: Arrange the apple slices in the air fryer basket in a single layer. You would need to do this in batches.

Step 4: Air fry for 14 to 15 minutes or until the apples are dry and crispy. Meanwhile, shake the basket two to three times during cooking.

Step 5: Remove the apple slices onto a platter to cool and serve after.

24. SPICED PECANS

Here's to not having your pecans bland again. This recipe shows you how to kick up the flavour for better enjoyment.

PREPARATION TIME: 20 MINUTES
COOKING TIME: 5 MINUTES
PER SERVING (4): KCAL: 387; FAT: 35.83G; CARBS: 12.72G; PROTEIN: 10.32G; SUGARS: 4.47G; FIBRE: 5.3G

INGREDIENTS:

- 2 cups pecans
- 1 tbsp. brown sugar
- 1 tbsp. soy sauce
- A pinch of ground cinnamon
- A pinch of cayenne pepper
- A pinch of salt

NSTRUCTIONS:

Step 1: Preheat the air fryer to 160°C.

Step 2: In a bowl, combine the pecans, brown sugar, soy sauce, cinnamon, cayenne pepper, and salt. Toss until the pecans are well coated with the seasoning. Let the pecans sit for 5 to 10 minutes.

Step 3: Line the air fryer basket with parchment paper and spoon the pecans on top. Toast them for 3 to 5 minutes or until the pecans are brown but not burned. Shake the basket halfway through cooking.

Step 4: Pour the pecans onto a baking tray and let them cool completely. Enjoy!

25. STRAWBERRY CHOCOLATE MUFFINS

Multiple levels of yumminess is what you get from these muffins. They smell great and can be enjoyed all day long. Serve them with juice for breakfast, have them as snacks, and even pair them with some ice cream as dessert.

PREPARATION TIME: 10 MINUTES
COOKING TIME: 20 MINUTES
PER SERVING (4): KCAL: 754; FAT: 38.06G; CARBS: 93.77G; PROTEIN: 10.74G; SUGARS: 48.96G; FIBRE: 5.3G

INGRENKEDIENTS:

For the dry ingredients:

- 335 g plain flour
- 60 g brown sugar
- 110 g granulated sugar
- 2 tsp. baking powder
- 1/2 tsp. ground cinnamon

For the wet ingredients:

- 2 large eggs
- 110 g melted unsalted butter
- 1 tsp. vanilla extract

For folding in:

- 225 g strawberries, diced
- 110 g mini chocolate chips

INSTRUCTIONS:

Step 1: Preheat the air fryer to 175ºC.

Step 2: For the dry ingredients, in a bowl, mix the flour, both sugars, baking powder, and cinnamon. For the wet ingredients, in another bowl, crack the eggs, and whisk with the butter, and vanilla extract. Gently whisk the dry mixture into the wet one until smooth batter forms. Add the strawberries and chocolate chips, and fold in well.

Step 3: Grease a four-cup muffin tin with cooking spray and pour in the batter two-thirds way up each tin.

Step 4: Put the muffin tin in the air fryer and bake for 15 to 20 minutes or until a toothpick inserted into each muffin comes out clean.

Step 5: Remove the tin from the air fryer and let the muffins cool in it for about 5 minutes. After, transfer them to a wire rack to cool to your desire.

Step 6: Serve the muffins.

SECTION 3.

STARTERS

**Don't Forget To Get The Color Images FREE!
Simply Scan The QR Code Below!**

Please scan the QR code below to access your bonus PDF with all 150 recipes with full coloured photos & beautiful designs alongside!

This is the only way we can get the recipes with coloured photos to you & keep the book as reasonably priced as possible.

Also, once downloaded you can take the PDF with you digitally wherever you go- meaning you can cook these recipes wherever you may be! (As long as you have an air fryer!)

We hope you enjoy and do let us know your feedback!

(INSERT QR CODE HERE)

STEP BY STEP Guide-
1. Open Your Phones (Or Any Device You Want The Book On) Back Camera. The Back Camera Is The One You use as if you are taking a picture of someone.
2. Simply point your Camera at the QR code and 'tap' the QR code with your finger to focus the camera.
3. A link / pop up will appear. Simply tap that (and make sure you have internet connection) and the FREE PDF containing all of the coloured images should appear.
4. Now you have access to these FOREVER. Simply 'Bookmark' The tab it opened on, or download the document and take wherever you want.
5. Repeat this on any device you want it on! (If you want it on a laptop, simply email the document to yourself!)

Any issues please email us at **vicandersonpublishing@gmail.com** and we will be happy to help!!

1. BACON CHICKEN ROLL UPS

Bacon chicken roll ups double as a starter and lunch option. They are an inviting set to whet appetites and could pair with sides like vegetables for a fuller meal.

PREPARATION TIME: 15 MINUTES
COOKING TIME: 15 MINUTES
PER SERVING (4): KCAL: 447; FAT: 29.73G; CARBS: 4.48G; PROTEIN: 39.02G; SUGARS: 1.07G; FIBRE: 0.3G

INGRENKEDIENTS:

- 2 chicken breasts
- 60g soft cheese, chopped, at room temperature
- 90g can creamed corn
- 40g cheese blend of choice
- 1 tbsp. chopped fresh coriander
- 4 bacon slices

INSTRUCTIONS:

Step 1: Preheat the air fryer to 180°C.

Step 2: Using a sharp knife, slice the chicken breasts in equal halves lengthwise, and use a rolling pin to gently pound them until they are flat.

Step 3: In a bowl, mix the soft cheese, creamed corn, cheese blend, and coriander. Spoon the mixture onto one end of each chicken piece and roll the chicken over the filling.

Step 4: After, roll each stuffed chicken in one bacon slice and use toothpicks to secure the ends. Sit the wrapped chicken in the air fryer and bake for 15 minutes or until the bacon is golden brown and the chicken reaches an internal temperature of 74°C.

Step 5: Remove the chicken onto a paper towel-lined plate to drain grease. Let rest for 5 to 10 minutes before slicing and serving.

2. BACON-WRAPPED AVOCADOS

Bacon-wrapped goods are always irresistible and these avocados are just scrumptious.

PREPARATION TIME: 10 MINUTES
COOKING TIME: 8 MINUTES
PER SERVING (4): KCAL: 186; FAT: 17.58G; CARBS: 4.5G; PROTEIN: 4.26G; SUGARS: 0.55G; FIBRE: 3.4G

INGREDIENTS:

- 1 large avocado
- 4 bacon slices

NSTRUCTIONS:

Step 1: Preheat the air fryer to 180°C.

Step 2: Cut the avocado in half, remove the pit, and peel it. Slice each half into 4 wedges to make 8 in total.

Step 3: Gently stretch the bacon until it is slightly elongated and cut it in half width wise. Wrap each bacon piece over each avocado and tuck the ends in.

Step 4: Place the wrapped avocado in the air fryer basket and air fry for 5 to 8 minutes or until the bacon is golden brown and cooked.

Step 5: Remove the wrapped avocados onto a paper towel-lined plate and let drain grease for about 2 minutes.

Step 6: Serve.

3. BREAD PIZZA STRIPS

Have you got any flatbread lurking around in your fridge? You can transform it into some bread strips that are loaded with cheese before it goes bad.

PREPARATION TIME: 10 MINUTES
COOKING TIME: 10 MINUTES
PER SERVING (4): KCAL: 80; FAT: 1.22G; CARBS: 6.79G; PROTEIN: 10.4G; SUGARS: 0.97G; FIBRE: 0.9G

INGRENKEDIENTS:

- 1 (18 cm diameter) flatbread
- 2 tbsp. pizza sauce
- 225 g grated mozzarella strips
- Chopped fresh basil for garnish

INSTRUCTIONS:

Step 1: Preheat the air fryer to 180°C.

Step 2: Lay the flatbread in the air fryer and spread the pizza sauce on top. After, spread the cheese all over it. (You can use a smaller sized flatbread if your air fryer is small. You would only need to double the recipe).

Step 3: Bake for 8 to 10 minutes or until the cheese melts.

Step 4: Remove the pizza onto a plate and slice it into strips.

Step 5: Garnish with basil and serve.

4. BREADED SHRIMP WITH SPICY MAYO

Breaded shrimp are the ultimate choice when thinking about starters for guests. Here, we pack them up with some spicy mayo for that needed kick of excitement.

PREPARATION TIME: 10 MINUTES
COOKING TIME: 10 MINUTES
PER SERVING (4): KCAL: 541; FAT: 46.74G; CARBS: 19.56G; PROTEIN: 9.67G; SUGARS: 1.17G; FIBRE: 0.9G

INGREDIENTS:

For the breaded shrimp:

- 16 large shrimp, peeled and deveined
- Salt and black pepper to taste
- 110 g plain flour
- 2 large eggs, beaten
- 225 g panko breadcrumbs

For the spicy mayo:

- 240 ml mayonnaise
- 1 tsp. hot sauce or to taste

NSTRUCTIONS:

For the breaded shrimp:

Step 1: Preheat the air fryer to 195°C.

Step 2: Season the shrimp with salt and black pepper.

Step 3: Dredge the shrimp in flour, dip them in eggs, and coat them in breadcrumbs.

Step 4: Mist the air fryer basket with cooking spray and put the shrimp in it. Air fry for 5 minutes per side or until the shrimp is golden brown.

Step 5: Remove the shrimp onto a plate.

For the spicy mayo:

Step 6: In a bowl, mix the mayonnaise and hot sauce until smooth.

Step 7: Serve the breaded shrimp with the spicy mayo.

5. CANDIED SWEET POTATO STACKERS

Your sweet tooth may just be satisfied by these sweet potato stackers. They double up on the sweetness and leave slightly punchy notes through each bite.

PREPARATION TIME: 15 MINUTES
COOKING TIME: 25 MINUTES
PER SERVING (4): KCAL: 1836; FAT: 188.75G; CARBS: 41.78G; PROTEIN: 4.1G; SUGARS: 26.28G; FIBRE: 3.8G

INGREDIENTS:

- 60 ml unsalted butter, melted
- 2 tbsp. maple syrup
- 60 g dark brown sugar
- 1 tsp. ground cinnamon
- 3 medium sweet potatoes
- 60 g finely chopped toasted pecans for topping

INSTRUCTIONS:

Step 1: Preheat the air fryer to 190°C.

Step 2: In a bowl, mix the butter, maple syrup, brown sugar, and cinnamon. Put it aside.

Step 3: Peel the sweet potatoes and starting at the shorter length, peel them into thin slices. Add the sweet potatoes to the butter mixture and toss to coat them well.

Step 4: In 8 to 12 muffin cups, stack the sweet potato slices one another until the cups are full.

Step 5: Place the cups in the air fryer and bake for 20 to 25 minutes or until the sweet potatoes are golden brown and cooked within.

Step 6: Remove the cups from the air fryer and empty the sweet potato stacks onto plates. Sprinkle the pecans on top of them.

Step 7: Serve them warm.

6. CHEESEBURGER ONION RINGS

This cheeseburger version is an upgraded version from the regular. You might not even taste the onions as they are rich with cheesy beef.

PREPARATION TIME: 15 MINUTES
COOKING TIME: 15 MINUTES
PER SERVING (4): KCAL: 502; FAT: 27G; CARBS: 29.57G; PROTEIN: 35.68G; SUGARS: 6.2G; FIBRE: 1.8G

INGREDIENTS:

- 450 g beef mince, 90% lean
- 2 tbsp. prepared mustard
- 80 ml ketchup
- A pinch of salt
- 1 large onion
- 110 g cheddar cheese, cut into 8 squares
- 170 g plain flour
- 2 tsp. garlic powder
- 2 large eggs, lightly beaten
- 335 g panko breadcrumbs

INSTRUCTIONS:

Step 1: Preheat the air fryer to 160°C.

Step 2: In a bowl, mix the beef mince, mustard, ketchup, and salt.

Step 3: Peel the onions and cut them into 1-cm-thick rings. Separate out 8 rings and keep the remaining onion for later use.

Step 4: Fill the 8 onion rings with half of the beef mixture, place a cheddar square on each, and cover with the remaining beef mixture. Mould the meat well to hold and cover the cheese.

Step 5: Mix the flour and garlic powder in a plate.

Step 6: Now, dredge the stuffed onion rings on both sides in the flour mixture, then in the eggs, and well coated in the breadcrumbs.

Step 7: Mist the air fryer basket with cooking spray and place the coated onion rings in it without overlapping. Mist their tops again with cooking spray and air fry for 12 to 15 minutes or until they are golden brown and the meat reaches an internal temperature of 63°C.

Step 8: Remove them onto a plate and let them rest for 5 to 10 minutes before serving.

7. CHEESY GARLIC BREAD

You can enjoy cheesy garlic bread as it is or pair it with soups on other days. It is a staple to make often with your air fryer.

PREPARATION TIME: 10 MINUTES
COOKING TIME: 10 MINUTES
PER SERVING (4): KCAL: 538; FAT: 17.48G; CARBS: 74.15G; PROTEIN: 21.62G; SUGARS: 6.67G; FIBRE: 3.2G

INGRENKEDIENTS:

- 1 baguette loaf
- 60 g salted butter, softened
- 1 tsp. garlic powder
- Salt and black pepper to taste
- 170 g grated mozzarella cheese
- 60 g grated Parmesan cheese
- 2 tsp. finely chopped fresh parsley

INSTRUCTIONS:

Step 1: Preheat the air fryer to 180°C.

Step 2: Split the baguette loaf in half lengthwise and cut each half into halves or thirds width wise.

Step 3: In a bowl, mix the butter, garlic powder, salt, and black pepper. Spread the garlic butter on the inner sides of the baguette pieces. Spread on the mozzarella cheese and Parmesan cheese.

Step 4: Place the bread in the air fryer and bake for 8 to 10 minutes or until the cheese melts.

Step 5: Remove the bread onto a plate and garnish with the parsley. Serve warm.

8. COURGETTE PIZZA FRITTERS

If you're looking to cut down on the carbs but still crave pizza now and then, these delicious mimicking fritters would do some satisfying.

PREPARATION TIME: 45 MINUTES
COOKING TIME: 20 MINUTES
PER SERVING (4): KCAL: 139; FAT: 4.97G; CARBS: 16.62G; PROTEIN: 7.31G; SUGARS: 0.92G; FIBRE: 1.8G

INGREDIENTS:

- 2 medium courgettes
- ½ small onion
- 1 medium potato, peeled
- 1 large egg, lightly beaten
- 30 g plain flour
- 110 g grated Parmesan cheese
- 1 tsp. onion powder
- 1 tsp. garlic powder
- 1/2 tsp. dried parsley flakes
- A pinch of salt
- 1 tsp. black pepper

NSTRUCTIONS:

Step 1: Into a bowl, coarsely grate the courgettes, onion, and potato. Add the egg, flour, Parmesan cheese, onion powder, garlic powder, dried parsley, salt, and black pepper. Mix well and form 6 cm size fritters from the mixture. Place the fritters in the fridge for 30 to 45 minutes.

Step 2: Preheat the air fryer to 200°C.

Step 3: Grease the air fryer basket with cooking spray and arrange the fritters in it in a single layer. Mist their tops with a little cooking spray.

Step 4: Air fry the fritters for 15 to 20 minutes or until golden brown and compacted.

Step 5: Remove them onto a plate and serve with marinara sauce.

9. CRANBERRY MEATBALLS

For Christmas or not? These cranberry meatballs are a unique way of packing them with a fruity flavour and creating a shiny, reddish, and sticky fill over them.

PREPARATION TIME: 15 MINUTES
COOKING TIME: 9 MINUTES
PER SERVING (4): KCAL: 429; FAT: 17.89G; CARBS: 42.11G; PROTEIN: 26.89G; SUGARS: 31.73G; FIBRE: 1.3G

INGREDIENTS:

For the meatballs:
- 450 g beef mince
- 1 large egg
- 2 tbsp. tomato puree, double concentrated
- 60 g finely chopped fresh parsley
- 60 g fine breadcrumbs
- 60 g finely grated Parmesan cheese
- Salt and black pepper to taste

For the sauce:
- 260 ml whole cranberry sauce
- 45 ml sweet chilli sauce
- 80 ml ketchup

INSTRUCTIONS:

Step 1: Preheat the air fryer to 200°C.

Step 2: In a bowl, combine the ingredients for the meatballs and mix them well. After, form 8 meatballs from the mixture.

Step 3: Grease the air fryer basket with cooking spray and add the meatballs. Mist their tops with cooking spray and air fry them for 6 to 7 minutes per side or until they are golden brown.

Step 4: Meanwhile, in a bowl, mix the cranberry sauce, sweet chilli sauce, and ketchup. Brush the sauce on the meatballs and cook them for 1 to 2 more minutes or until the sauce feels sticky on the meatballs.

Step 5: Transfer them to a plate, let them rest for 5 minutes, and serve them warm.

10. CRISPY MOZZARELLA RICE BALLS

In Italy, these rice balls are called arancini. This recipe mimics that recipe with the assumption that you may have some leftover cooked rice in the fridge and could remodel them into some cheesy balls.

PREPARATION TIME: 15 MINUTES
COOKING TIME: 10 MINUTES
PER SERVING (4): KCAL: 357; FAT: 11.9G; CARBS: 44.6G; PROTEIN: 16.19G; SUGARS: 2.77G; FIBRE: 2G

INGREDIENTS:

- 225 g cooked short-grain rice
- 1 tbsp. dry white wine or cider vinegar
- 1/2 tsp. garlic powder
- 1/2 tsp. onion powder
- 110 g freshly grated Parmesan cheese
- Salt and black pepper to taste
- 110 g + 45 g herb-seasoned breadcrumbs
- 15 (1 cm) cubes mozzarella cheese

INSTRUCTIONS:

Step 1: Preheat the air fryer to 200°C.

Step 2: In a bowl, mix the rice, white wine or cider vinegar, garlic powder, onion powder, Parmesan, salt, and black pepper. Stir through 45 g of the breadcrumbs.

Step 3: Next, form 15 equal size balls from the mixture and press one mozzarella cube into each one. Roll each rice portion in your hands into a bowl, making sure the rice covers the cheese. After, roll each ball in the remaining breadcrumbs until well-coated.

Step 4: Mist the air fryer basket with cooking spray and place the balls in it. Mist them again with cooking spray and air fry for 10 minutes, while shaking the basket halfway through cooking. When they are golden brown and crispy, they are ready.

Step 5: Remove them onto a plate and serve them with your favourite dipping sauce.

11. CRUNCHY CHICKEN STRIPS

Serve these chicken strips with your favourite dipping sauce, over salad, or even with potato chips. They are so versatile.

PREPARATION TIME: 10 MINUTES
COOKING TIME: 16 MINUTES
PER SERVING (4): KCAL: 370; FAT: 16.53G; CARBS: 16.64G; PROTEIN: 36.17G; SUGARS: 0.64G; FIBRE: 0.7G

INGREDIENTS:

- 2 chicken breasts, skinless and boneless
- Salt and black pepper to taste
- 110 g plain flour
- 2 large eggs, beaten
- 225 g seasoned breadcrumbs

INSTRUCTIONS:

Step 1: Preheat the air fryer to 200°C.

Step 2: Cut the chicken breasts in halves lengthwise and then, cut each half into two strips. Pat them dry with paper towels and season with salt and black pepper on both sides.

Step 3: Dredge the chicken in flour, dip them in eggs, and coat them in the breadcrumbs.

Step 4: Mist the air fryer basket with cooking spray and lay the chicken in it. Mist their tops with cooking spray and air fry for 5 to 8 minutes per side or until the chicken is golden brown and reaches an internal temperature of 74°C.

Step 5: Remove the chicken onto a plate and serve with your favourite dipping sauce.

12. CRUNCHY PICKLES

After this recipe, I am certain you won't have regular pickles anymore. Breading them gives them a better crunch and depth of flavour.

PREPARATION TIME: 10 MINUTES
COOKING TIME: 12 MINUTES
PER SERVING (4): KCAL: 203; FAT: 4.05G; CARBS: 32.21G; PROTEIN: 8.5G; SUGARS: 2.11G; FIBRE: 1.9G

INGREDIENTS:

- 16 thick pickles slices
- 110 g plain flour
- 2 large eggs, beaten
- 225 g seasoned breadcrumbs

INSTRUCTIONS:

Step 1: Preheat the air fryer to 200°C.

Step 2: Pat the pickles dry on both sides with paper towels.

Step 3: Dredge the pickles in flour, dip them in eggs, and coat well in the breadcrumbs.

Step 4: Mist the air fryer basket with cooking spray and lay the pickles in it in a single layer. Mist their tops with cooking spray and air fry for 4 to 6 minutes per side or until they are golden brown and crispy.

Step 5: Plate the crunchy pickles and enjoy them.

13. FETA AND FIG MEATBALLS

I love both ingredients used for the meatballs here—feta and fig jam. They add sweetness, saltiness, and tang to the meatballs and make them stand out.

PREPARATION TIME: 15 MINUTES
COOKING TIME: 16 MINUTES
PER SERVING (4): KCAL: 277; FAT: 16.28G; CARBS: 4.77G; PROTEIN: 27.75G; SUGARS: 3.28G; FIBRE: 0.2G

INGRENKEDIENTS:

- 450 g turkey mince
- 140 g feta cheese, crumbled
- 1 tsp. ground cumin
- 1 tsp. garlic powder
- Salt and black pepper to taste
- 160 ml fig jam
- 1 tbsp. apple cider vinegar
- 1 tbsp. fish sauce

INSTRUCTIONS:

Step 1: Preheat the air fryer to 200°C.

Step 2: In a bowl, mix the turkey, feta cheese, cumin, garlic powder, salt, and black pepper. Form 8 meatballs from the mixture.

Step 3: Grease the air fryer basket with cooking spray and add the meatballs. Mist their tops with cooking spray and air fry them for 6 to 7 minutes per side or until they are golden brown.

Step 4: Meanwhile, in a bowl, mix the fig jam, apple cider vinegar, and fish sauce. Brush the sauce on the meatballs and cook them for 1 to 2 more minutes or until the sauce feels sticky on the meatballs.

Step 5: Transfer them to a plate, let them rest for 5 minutes, and serve them warm.

14. FRESH CRAB CAKES

I use imitation crab meat on some days but I prefer the fresh meat. Eating crabs can be cumbersome, so this recipe creates a more pleasing way to enjoy them without the battle with their shells.

PREPARATION TIME: 10 MINUTES
COOKING TIME: 12 MINUTES
PER SERVING (4): KCAL: 115; FAT: 11.5G; CARBS: 18.7G; PROTEIN: 12.21G; SUGARS: 2.6G; FIBRE: 1.4G

INGREDIENTS:

- 225 g fresh crabmeat
- 2 green onions, chopped
- 60 g red bell pepper, chopped
- 2 tbsp. mayonnaise
- 1 tbsp. yellow mustard
- 30 g breadcrumbs
- Lemon wedges for serving

INSTRUCTIONS:

Step 1: Preheat the air fryer to 175°C.

Step 2: Add all the ingredients to a bowl except for lemon wedges. Mix them well and form four patties from the mixture.

Step 3: Mist the air fryer basket with cooking spray and add the patties to it in a single layer. Mist their tops with cooking spray and cook for 5 to 6 minutes per side or until they are golden brown.

Step 4: Remove them onto a plate, squeeze on some lemon juice, and serve with the remaining lemon wedges.

15. CHILLI GARLIC BREAD

This garlic bread packs some heat for those days when you're feeling spicy.

PREPARATION TIME: 10 MINUTES
COOKING TIME: 8 MINUTES
PER SERVING (4): KCAL: 509; FAT: 16.64G; CARBS: 73.72G; PROTEIN: 17.01G; SUGARS: 6.46G; FIBRE: 3.2G

INGRENKEDIENTS:

- 1 baguette loaf
- 60 g salted butter, softened
- 1 small red chilli, deseeded and finely minced
- 1 tsp. garlic powder
- 60 g grated Parmesan cheese
- Salt and black pepper to taste
- 2 tsp. finely chopped fresh parsley

INSTRUCTIONS:

Step 1: Preheat the air fryer to 180°C.

Step 2: Slice the baguette into 1 cm pieces.

Step 3: In a bowl, mix the butter, red chilli, garlic powder, Parmesan cheese, salt, and black pepper. Brush the mixture on both sides of the bread slices.

Step 4: Place the bread in the air fryer without overlapping and bake for 3 to 4 minutes per side or until they are golden brown.

Step 5: Plate them, garnish with parsley, and serve warm.

16. HONEYED DRUMSTICKS

By simply tossing some chicken drumsticks in honey, you elevate their tastes. They aren't fussy at all.

PREPARATION TIME: 10 MINUTES
COOKING TIME: 15 MINUTES
PER SERVING (4): KCAL: 183; FAT: 7.08G; CARBS: 3.21; PROTEIN: 25.3G; SUGARS: 2.9G; FIBRE: 0.1G

INGREDIENTS:

- 4 chicken drumsticks, skinless and bone-in
- Salt and black pepper to taste
- 2 tsp. olive oil
- 2 tsp. honey
- 1/2 tsp. minced garlic

NSTRUCTIONS:

Step 1: Preheat the air fryer to 200°C.

Step 2: Season the drumsticks and add them to a bowl.

Step 3: Mix the olive oil, honey, and garlic and pour it over the chicken. Toss well and cover the bowl. Let the chicken marinate for 30 minutes.

Step 4: Lay the chicken in the air fryer without overlapping and air fry for 7 to 10 minutes per side or until the chicken is golden brown and the thicker side reaches an internal temperature of 74°C.

Step 5: Take out the chicken onto a plate, let rest for 5 to 10 minutes, and serve.

17. MINI PORK SLIDERS

You'll nearly always find pork sliders at any party. So, here is your winning pass to make them the best.

PREPARATION TIME: 60 MINUTES
COOKING TIME: 23 MINUTES
PER SERVING (24): KCAL: 154; FAT: 3.63G; CARBS: 20.68G; PROTEIN: 9.02G; SUGARS: 1.42G; FIBRE: 0.8G

INGREDIENTS:

For the mini buns:
- 1 kg plain flour, plus extra for dusting
- 1 (7 g) package instant yeast
- 30 g granulated sugar
- 1.5 tsp. salt
- 1 egg

For the pulled pork filling:
- 450 g pork chops, boneless
- Salt and black pepper to taste
- 120 ml BBQ sauce
- 1 tsp. Worcestershire sauce
- 1 tsp. onion flakes

For the sliders:
- 6 slices provolone cheese, cut into 24 equal squares
- 60 g butter, melted
- 1 tsp. poppy seeds (optional)

INSTRUCTIONS:

For the mini buns:
Step 1: In a bowl, mix the flour, yeast, sugar, and salt. Crack in the egg and mix until rough dough comes together. Dust a clean, working surface with flour and knead the dough a few times until smooth and stretchy.
Step 2: Divide the dough into 24 equal balls and flatten each one slightly. Put the dough balls on a baking sheet, cover with a clean napkin, and leave to rise for 30 minutes.
Step 3: Preheat the air fryer to 200°C.
Step 4: Working in batches, place some dough balls in the air fryer basket and bake for 10 minutes or until they are golden brown and risen.
Step 5: Remove them onto a wire rack to cool while you prepare the pork filling.

For the pulled pork filling:
Step 6: Season the pork with salt and black pepper, and mist it on both sides with cooking spray.
Step 7: Put the pork in the air fryer basket and cook at 200°C for 10 to 12 minutes or until it reaches an internal temperature of 63°C.
Step 8: Remove the pork onto a plate and let it rest for 10 minutes. After, using two forks, shred the pork into tiny bits. Add the shredded pork to a bowl.
Step 9: Onto the pork, add the BBQ sauce, Worcestershire sauce, and onion flakes. Mix well.

For the sliders:
Step 10: Slice the buns in halves width wise.
Step 11: On the bottom parts of the buns, add one cheese piece and spoon some of the pork mixture on it. Cover the fillings with the top parts of the buns and brush them with butter. Sprinkle on some poppy seeds if using.
Step 12: Place the buns in the air fryer and warm at 175°C for 1 minute or until the cheeses melt. You may need to do this part in batches.
Step 13: Arrange the sliders on a serving platter and serve.

18. MUSHROOMS WITH SAGE AND ONION STUFFING

Making stuffing is rather simpler than thought and this recipe gives you all the confidence you need to make them excellently.

PREPARATION TIME: 10 MINUTES
COOKING TIME: 10 MINUTES
PER SERVING (4): KCAL: 539; FAT: 17.5 G; CARBS: 79.22G; PROTEIN: 15.5 G; SUGARS: 7.59G; FIBRE: 5.1G

INGREDIENTS:

- 4 cups herb seasoned breadcrumbs
- 360 ml chicken or vegetable broth
- 60 ml butter, melted
- 110 g chopped white mushrooms
- 60 g chopped onion
- 1 tsp. dried sage

INSTRUCTIONS:

Step 1: Preheat the air fryer to 160°C.
Step 2: In a bowl, mix the breadcrumbs and chicken or vegetable broth.
Step 3: Stir in the butter, mushrooms, onion, and sage until well combined.
Step 4: Line the air fryer basket with parchment paper, mist with cooking spray, and spread the stuffing mixture in it. Cook for 8 to 10 minutes while stirring through once or twice during cooking until the stuffing is golden brown and the mushrooms are cooked.
Step 5: Spoon the stuffing into a bowl and let cool before serving.

19. PANCETTA-WRAPPED ASPARAGUS

Mostly, asparagus is wrapped with bacon and enjoyed. I find pancetta to be a fine alternative that cuts down on the punchy notes just a little bit while giving you other options to work with.

PREPARATION TIME: 10 MINUTES
COOKING TIME: 8 MINUTES
PER SERVING (4): KCAL: 107; FAT: 10.22G; CARBS: 0.49G; PROTEIN: 3.41G; SUGARS: 0.35G; FIBRE: 0.1G

INGREDIENTS:

- 8 small asparagus spears, hard stems trimmed
- 4 bacon slices, each halved width wise

INSTRUCTIONS:

Step 1: Preheat the air fryer to 180°C.

Step 2: Gently stretch the bacon until it is slightly elongated and cut it in half width wise.

Step 3: Wrap each asparagus from one end to the other with one bacon piece and tuck the ends in.

Step 3: Place the asparagus in the air fryer basket and air fry for 5 to 8 minutes or until the bacon is golden brown and the asparagus cooked.

Step 4: Remove the wrapped asparagus onto a paper towel-lined plate to drain its grease for about 2 minutes.

Step 5: Plate them and serve.

20. POPCORN CHICKEN

If you've got kids, you can make these mini chicken bites for them and earn yourself some cute kisses for the day. Adults will enjoy these too.

PREPARATION TIME: 15 MINUTES
COOKING TIME: 12 MINUTES
PER SERVING (4): KCAL: 398; FAT: 13.92G; CARBS: 34.83G; PROTEIN: 31.49G; SUGARS: 2.7G; FIBRE: 2.5G

INGREDIENTS:

- 450 g chicken breasts, boneless, skinless
- Salt and black pepper to taste
- 30 g plain flour
- 1 large egg
- 330 g panko breadcrumbs
- 2 tsp. onion powder
- 2 tsp. garlic powder
- 1 tsp. dried oregano

INSTRUCTIONS:

Step 1: Preheat the air fryer to 400°C.

Step 2: Cut the chicken into 2 cm pieces and season with salt and black pepper.

Step 3: Pour the flour on a plate, beat the egg, and on another plate, mix the breadcrumbs, onion powder, garlic powder, oregano, a little salt, and black pepper.

Step 4: Dip each chicken piece in the flour, then in egg, and coat well with the breadcrumb mixture.

Step 5: Mist the air fryer basket with cooking spray, add the chicken, and mist again with cooking spray.

Step 6: Air fry the chicken for 10 to 12 minutes while shaking the basket halfway until they are golden brown and the chicken is cooked within.

Step 7: Remove the chicken onto a plate, let rest for 5 minutes, and serve with your favourite dipping sauce.

21. SHRIMP CAKE SLIDERS

An exciting way to serve some shrimp is in shrimp cakes. Loading them in mini sliders also makes them quite filling.

PREPARATION TIME: 30 MINUTES
COOKING TIME: 8 MINUTES
PER SERVING (12): KCAL: 216; FAT: 10.59G; CARBS: 21.58G; PROTEIN: 8.66G; SUGARS: 8.22G; FIBRE: 1.7G

INGRENKEDIENTS:

- 450 g large shrimp, peeled and deveined
- 1 large egg, lightly beaten
- 6 green onions, chopped
- 110 g finely chopped red sweet pepper
- 1 tbsp. finely minced fresh ginger
- 225 g panko breadcrumbs
- A pinch of salt to taste
- 60 ml mayonnaise
- 1 tsp. hot sauce
- 1 tbsp. sweet chilli sauce
- A few leaves of shredded cabbage
- 12 mini buns, split

INSTRUCTIONS:

Step 1: Preheat the air fryer to 190°C.

Step 2: Add the shrimp to a food processor and process until coarsely smooth. Add the shrimp to a bowl and mix with the egg, half of the green onions, red sweet pepper, ginger, breadcrumbs, and salt. Form 12 equal patties from the mixture and refrigerate them for 20 minutes.

Step 3: Mist the air fryer basket with cooking spray, lay in the shrimp patties, and mist their tops with cooking spray. Air fry them for 5 to 8 minutes or until they are golden brown.

Step 4: Meanwhile, in a bowl, mix the mayonnaise, hot sauce, and sweet chilli sauce. Add the cabbage and green onions, and mix well.

Step 5: When the shrimp cakes are ready, remove them onto a plate and toast the buns in the air fryer for 1 minute or until they are golden brown.

Step 6: Remove the buns and place one shrimp cake on each bottom bun. Spoon the cabbage mixture on top and cover with the top buns.

Step 7: Serve the sliders.

22. SPINACH AND GOAT CHEESE TURNOVERS

These are delicious vegetarian options to serve at your next party with friends. They pack a lot of flavour, texture, and taste.

PREPARATION TIME: 10 MINUTES
COOKING TIME: 18 MINUTES
PER SERVING (8): KCAL: 143; FAT: 9.61G; CARBS: 8.47G; PROTEIN: 6.99G; SUGARS: 0.48G; FIBRE: 2G

INGREDIENTS:

- 2 tsp. olive oil
- 2 bunches English spinach, ends trimmed, washed, and chopped
- 2 eggs
- Salt and black pepper to taste
- 100 g crumbled goat cheese
- 2 sheets (25 x 25cm) frozen puff pastry, just thawed

NSTRUCTIONS:

Step 1: Preheat the air fryer to 180°C.

Step 2: Heat the olive oil in a skillet over medium heat (on a stovetop) and cook in the spinach for 3 minutes or until it has wilted. Let the spinach cool.

Step 3: Crack one egg into a bowl, lightly whisk, and mix in the spinach and goat cheese. Season lightly with salt and black pepper.

Step 4: Divide each pastry sheet into four equals. Crack the egg into a small bowl and lightly beat.

Step 5: Divide the spinach onto the centre of each pastry piece. Brush the edges of the pastry with egg and fold each one over the filling in half diagonally. Press the edges to seal.

Step 6: Mist the air fryer basket with cooking spray. Working in batches, add some of the filled pastries to the basket and mist their tops with cooking spray.

Step 7: Bake for 10 to 15 minutes or until they are golden brown and puffed up.

Step 8: Remove them onto a wire rack to slightly cool and serve them.

23. THIN GINGER BEEF SKEWERS

Enjoy these gingery beef skewers as a rewarding treat. The beef pieces are thin for comfortable bites.

PREPARATION TIME: 50 MINUTES
COOKING TIME: 8 MINUTES
PER SERVING (4): KCAL: 229; FAT: 9.5G; CARBS: 19.97G; PROTEIN: 30.52G; SUGARS: 14G; FIBRE: 0.7G

INGREDIENTS:

- 450 g beef flank steak
- 240 ml soy sauce
- 240 ml rice vinegar
- 1 tbsp. sesame oil
- 60 g packed brown sugar
- 6 garlic cloves, minced
- 2 tbsp. minced fresh ginger
- 1 tsp. hot sauce
- ½ tsp. corn flour
- Small metal skewers for threading, pre-soaked
- Sesame seeds and chopped green onions for garnish

INSTRUCTIONS:

Step 1: Thinly cut the beef into 0.5-cm-long strips. In a wide bowl, mix the soy sauce, rice vinegar, sesame oil, brown sugar, garlic, ginger, hot sauce, and corns flour. Preserve about a third of the marinade for later use.

Step 2: Add the beef to the remaining marinade and mix well. Cover the bowl and place it in the fridge for 30 minutes. This will marinate the beef and infuse it with the ginger flavour.

Step 3: Preheat the air fryer to 400°C.

Step 4: Remove the bowl from the fridge and thread the beef on the skewers, about one long strip of beef to one small skewer.

Step 5: Grease the air fryer with cooking spray and arrange the skewers in it. Mist them with cooking spray and "grill" for 3 minutes per side. Baste the beef with the reserved marinade on both sides and cook for 1 to 2 more minutes or until the beef reaches your desired doneness.

Step 6: Remove the beef onto a plate, garnish with sesame seeds and green onions, and let rest for 5 minutes.

Step 7: Serve the beef skewers warm.

24. TURKEY AND CHEDDAR QUESADILLAS

If you've got some leftover turkey or chicken in your fridge, making these quesadillas would be handy. The recipe requires only three ingredients to appreciate using leftovers.

PREPARATION TIME: 5 MINUTES
COOKING TIME: 8 MINUTES
PER SERVING (4): KCAL: 216; FAT: 8.33G; CARBS: 12.22G; PROTEIN: 21.74G; SUGARS: 0.82G; FIBRE: 0.6G

INGREDIENTS:

- 2 flour tortillas (medium size or good size for your air fryer space)
- 110 g cheddar cheese or more if needed
- 110 g precooked or leftover turkey, shredded

Topping options:

- Soured cream
- Salsa
- Chopped coriander leaves

INSTRUCTIONS:

Step 1: Preheat the air fryer to 175°C.

Step 2: Mist the air fryer basket with cooking spray and lay one tortilla in it. Spread half of the cheese on it, top with the turkey, and spread the remaining cheese on top. Cover with the other tortilla and lightly mist their tops with cooking spray.

Step 3: Bake for 4 minutes, carefully flip them, and bake for another 4 minutes or until the tortillas are golden brown and the cheese melted.

Step 4: Remove the quesadilla onto a plate and cut into four equal triangles.

Step 5: Serve ahead.

25. WINTERY ROLLS WITH SWEET CHILLI DIP

You will love how these colourful rolls light up your mood once broken into. And they always pair well with sweet chilli sauce.

PREPARATION TIME: 10 MINUTES
COOKING TIME: 21 MINUTES
PER SERVING (4): KCAL: 325; FAT: 24.81G; CARBS: 21.43G; PROTEIN: 3.9G; SUGARS: 1.36G; FIBRE: 0.8G

INGRENKEDIENTS:

For the wintery rolls:

- 2 tbsp. olive oil
- 110 g thinly shredded red cabbage
- 1 carrot, cut into thin strips
- 110 g bean sprouts
- 1 tsp. finely minced ginger
- 1 tsp. minced garlic
- 1 tbsp. chopped fresh mint
- Salt and black pepper to taste
- 8 square spring roll wrappers

For the sweet chilli dip:

- 240 ml mayonnaise
- 2 tbsp. sweet chilli sauce or to taste

INSTRUCTIONS:

For the wintery rolls:

Step 1: Preheat the air fryer to 200°C.

Step 2: Heat the olive oil in a skillet over medium heat (on a stovetop). Add the vegetables and sauté them for 5 minutes or until they are tender. Stir in the ginger, garlic, mint, salt, and black pepper. Cook for 1 minute and turn the heat off.

Step 3: Divide the mixture onto the spring roll wrappers. Fold two opposite sides of the wrappers over the filling. Dip your finger in water and brush the edges of the other two sides with it. Fold these other sides over the filling and gently run your finger around the edges to seal.

Step 4: Grease the air fryer basket with cooking spray, lay in the rolls without overlapping them, and mist their tops with cooking spray. Air fry them for 5 minutes per side or until they are golden brown.

Step 5: Remove them onto a plate to cool slightly.

For the sweet chilli dip:

Step 6: Meanwhile, in a bowl, mix the mayonnaise and sweet chilli sauce.

Step 7: Serve the wintery rolls with the sweet chilli sauce.

SECTION 4.

LUNCH

Don't Forget To Get The Color Images FREE!
Simply Scan The QR Code Below!

Please scan the QR code below to access your bonus PDF with all 150 recipes with full coloured photos & beautiful designs alongside!

This is the only way we can get the recipes with coloured photos to you & keep the book as reasonably priced as possible.

Also, once downloaded you can take the PDF with you digitally wherever you go- meaning you can cook these recipes wherever you may be! (As long as you have an air fryer!)

We hope you enjoy and do let us know your feedback!

(INSERT QR CODE HERE)

STEP BY STEP Guide-

1. Open Your Phones (Or Any Device You Want The Book On) Back Camera. The Back Camera Is The One You use as if you are taking a picture of someone.
2. Simply point your Camera at the QR code and 'tap' the QR code with your finger to focus the camera.
3. A link / pop up will appear. Simply tap that (and make sure you have internet connection) and the FREE PDF containing all of the coloured images should appear.
4. Now you have access to these FOREVER. Simply 'Bookmark' The tab it opened on, or download the document and take wherever you want.
5. Repeat this on any device you want it on! (If you want it on a laptop, simply email the document to yourself!)

Any issues please email us at **vicandersonpublishing@gmail.com** and we will be happy to help!!

1. BAKED BUTTERY POTATOES

Buttery potatoes are naturally creamy, so when tossed with some butter and seasoning, they turn out to be an amazing side dish for many foods.

PREPARATION TIME: 10 MINUTES
COOKING TIME: 20 MINUTES
PER SERVING (4): KCAL: 187; FAT: 5.97G; CARBS: 30.74G; PROTEIN: 3.73G; SUGARS: 1.41G; FIBRE: 4G

INGRENKEDIENTS:

- 680 g baby butter potatoes
- 2 tbsp. melted butter
- 1/2 tsp. onion powder
- 1 tsp. garlic powder
- 1/2 tsp. paprika
- 1 tsp. salt
- Fresh minced parsley for serving

INSTRUCTIONS:

Step 1: Preheat the air fryer to 200°C.

Step 2: Peel the potatoes, cut them into bite-size chunks, and add them to a bowl.

Step 3: Drizzle on the butter and top with the onion powder, garlic powder, paprika, and salt. Toss well.

Step 4: Add the potatoes to the air fryer basket and bake for 18 to 20 minutes or until the potatoes are golden and tender. Meanwhile, shake the basket every 5 minutes during cooking.

Step 5: Spoon the potatoes onto a serving platter and garnish with parsley.

Step 6: Serve warm.

2. BEEF AND PORK BELLY LETTUCE WRAPS

I love pairing these lettuce wraps with some rice or quinoa on those days when I am really hungry. Otherwise, they are great as they are or topped with shredded vegetables.

PREPARATION TIME: 10 MINUTES
COOKING TIME: 9 MINUTES
PER SERVING (4): KCAL: 313; FAT: 20.78G; CARBS: 9.53G; PROTEIN: 21.76G; SUGARS: 6.85G; FIBRE: 0.8G

INGREDIENTS:

For the lettuce wraps:
- 225 g beef mince
- 225 g pork mince
- 1 small yellow onion, diced
- Butterhead lettuce leaves for serving
- Chopped green onions for topping

For the sauce:
- 2 tbsp. soy sauce
- 1 tbsp. honey
- 1 tbsp. rice wine vinegar
- 2 tsp. fresh ground ginger
- 2 garlic cloves, minced
- 1 tsp. hot sauce or to taste

INSTRUCTIONS:

Step 1: Preheat the air fryer to 200°C.

Step 2: In an air fryer-safe baking dish, combine the beef mince, pork mince, and onion. Place the dish in the air fryer and cook for 7 to 8 minutes or until the meat is mostly brown. Meanwhile, stir twice during cooking.

Step 3: At the same time, combine all the ingredients for the sauce into a pot and cook on your stovetop over medium heat for 2 to 4 minutes or until the sauce slightly thickens.

Step 4: Drizzle about 2 tbsp. of the sauce on the meat and stir well. Cook for 1 more minute in the air fryer. Remove the baking pan when ready.

Step 5: Spoon the meat into the lettuce leaves, top with some green onions, and serve with the remaining sauce.

The UK Air Fryer Cookbook for Beginners

3. BEER-BATTERED HADDOCK WITH SWEDE CHIPS

You'll love how delicious these light and hearty fish pieces pair with swedes. Swedes contain very little amounts of carbohydrates and are a great alternative to potatoes.

PREPARATION TIME: 15 MINUTES
COOKING TIME: 12 MINUTES
PER SERVING (4): KCAL: 410; FAT: 2.56G; CARBS: 51.18G; PROTEIN: 39.35G; SUGARS: 2.54G; FIBRE: 2.8G

INGRENKEDIENTS:

For the beer-battered haddock:
- 400 g plain flour
- 30 g corn flour
- 1/2 tsp. baking soda
- 175 ml beer
- 1 egg beaten
- 1/2 tsp. paprika
- A pinch of cayenne pepper
- 1 tsp. salt
- A pinch of black pepper
- 4 haddock fillets

For the swede chips:
- 2 swedes, peeled and cut into 3 cm strips
- Salt to taste

INSTRUCTIONS:

Step 1: Preheat the air fryer to 180°C.

Step 2: In a bowl, mix 150 g of plain flour, corn flour, baking soda, and beer until smooth. Pour the egg onto a plate and in another plate, mix the remaining flour, paprika, cayenne pepper, salt, and black pepper.

Step 3: Pat the haddock dry with paper towels. Dredge the fish in the dry flour mix, then dip them in the eggs, and then in the beer batter.

Step 4: Line the air fryer with parchment paper, mist it with cooking spray, and lay the battered fish on top. Also, add the swede pieces to the side of them. You may need to do this in two equal batches if your cooking space is small.

Step 5: Air fry for 12 minutes or until the fish is golden brown and flaky within, and the swede golden brown and cooked within.

Step 6: Remove the fish onto a plate to rest. Add the swede to a plate, season with a little salt, and toss well.

Step 7. Serve the battered fish with the swede chips.

4. BUBBLE AND SQUEAK CAKES

This classic and no-time-wasting British side dish is one of my favourites ever because it makes good use of leftovers that I may have in the fridge and is also quick to assemble.

PREPARATION TIME: 5 MINUTES
COOKING TIME: 12 MINUTES
PER SERVING (4): KCAL: 214; FAT: 5.5G; CARBS: 30.23G; PROTEIN: 11.6G; SUGARS: 3.75G; FIBRE: 3.3G

INGREDIENTS:

- 500 g leftover mashed potatoes
- 200 g shredded cabbage, steamed in the microwave
- 100 g leftover beef mince
- 2 tsp. chopped fresh thyme
- Salt and black pepper to taste
- 30 g grated cheddar cheese

NSTRUCTIONS:

Step 1: Preheat the air fryer to 200°C.

Step 2: In a bowl, mix the potatoes, cabbage, beef mince, thyme, salt, black pepper, and cheddar cheese.

Step 3: Add the mixture to 4 medium ramekins and level their tops.

Step 4: Put the ramekins in the air fryer and bake for 10 to 12 minutes or until the top is golden brown.

Step 5: Remove the ramekins from the air fryer, invert the cakes onto serving plates, and serve warm.

5. CHICKEN PARMESAN

Parmesan adds a kick to chicken. Have a go at making this simple but tasty delicacy.

PREPARATION TIME: 15 MINUTES
COOKING TIME: 13 MINUTES
PER SERVING (4): KCAL: 664; FAT: 12.7G; CARBS: 16.88G; PROTEIN: 115.02G; SUGARS: 3.92G; FIBRE: 2.5G

INGRENKEDIENTS:

- 4 (170 g) chicken breasts, skinless and boneless
- Salt and black pepper to taste
- 2 large eggs
- 110 g seasoned breadcrumbs
- 75 g grated Parmesan cheese
- 240 ml pasta sauce
- 225 g grated mozzarella cheese
- Chopped fresh basil for garnish

INSTRUCTIONS:

Step 1: Preheat the air fryer to 200°C.

Step 2: Cut the chicken breasts in halves.

Step 3: Crack the eggs into a bowl and lightly beat. On a plate, mix the breadcrumbs, half of the Parmesan cheese, and pinch of black pepper.

Step 4: Dip the chicken in the eggs and coat well with the breadcrumb mixture.

Step 5: Mist the air fryer with cooking spray and lay in the chicken in the air fryer basket. Cook for 10 to 12 minutes or until the chicken is golden brown and reaches an internal temperature of 74°C.

Step 6: Spoon the pasta sauce onto the chicken and spread the mozzarella cheese on top. Bake for 1 more minute or until the cheese has melted.

Step 7: Remove the chicken onto a plate, garnish with basil, sprinkle on the remaining Parmesan, and serve warm with pasta.

6. CHILI LIME CHICKEN WITH PEPPERS

They pack a punch of aroma and tang that would serve well in wraps, over rice, or with potatoes.

PREPARATION TIME: 10 MINUTES
COOKING TIME: 12 MINUTES
PER SERVING (4): KCAL: 216; FAT: 9.03G; CARBS: 7.4G; PROTEIN: 26.35G; SUGARS: 1.65G; FIBRE: 1.7G

INGREDIENTS:

- 450 g chicken thighs, boneless and skinless
- 1 red bell pepper, deseeded and thinly sliced
- 1 yellow bell pepper, deseeded and thinly sliced
- 2 tbsp. olive oil
- 60 ml lime juice
- 2 tsp. chilli powder
- 1 tsp. garlic powder
- 1/2 tsp. paprika
- Salt to taste

NSTRUCTIONS:

Step 1: Preheat the air fryer to 190°C.

Step 2: Cut the chicken into thin strips and add them to a bowl along with the bell peppers. Add the olive oil, lime juice, chilli powder, garlic powder, paprika, and salt. Toss well.

Step 3: Add the chicken and peppers to the air fryer basket. Cook for 10 to 12 minutes or until golden brown, the peppers tender, and chicken cooked through.

Step 4: Spoon the chicken and peppers onto a plate and serve warm with rice or in wraps.

7. COURGETTES AND CHICORY WITH OLIVE DRESSING

This dish actually goes beyond courgettes packed in chicory leaves. It accommodates other vegetables as well so you can reap as many nutrients from one dish while getting enticed by a colourful display.

PREPARATION TIME: 10 MINUTES
COOKING TIME: 10 MINUTES
PER SERVING (4): KCAL: 292; FAT: 29.03G; CARBS: 9.25G; PROTEIN: 1.72G; SUGARS: 2.64G; FIBRE: 1.4G

INGREDIENTS:

For the vegetables:
- 1 courgette, thinly sliced
- Other vegetables to add (sliced peppers, cherry tomatoes, sliced yellow squash, sliced red onions, etc.)
- 1 tbsp. olive oil
- Salt to taste

For the olive oil dressing:
- 120 ml extra virgin olive oil
- 240 ml fresh lemon juice
- 8 garlic cloves, minced
- 4 tsp. salt
- ½ tsp. black pepper

For serving:
- Chicory leaves

INSTRUCTIONS:

For the vegetables:

Step 1: Preheat the air fryer to 180°C.

Step 2: In a bowl, add the courgettes and any other soft cooking vegetables of choice. Toss them with olive oil and salt.

Step 3: Add the vegetables to the air fryer and cook for 7 to 10 minutes or until they are tender.

Step 4: Remove the vegetables into a bowl.

For the olive oil dressing:

Step 5: In a small jar, add the olive oil, lemon juice, garlic, salt, and black pepper. Cover the jar and shake to mix well.

Step 6: Drizzle the olive oil dressing over the vegetables (to your taste) and toss well.

Step 7: Spoon the vegetables into the chicory leaves and serve.

8. CRUNCHY PARSLEY CROUTONS

You will need these croutons for many servings. You can have them over soups, topped on salad, enjoyed as a snack with dipping sauce, or used for stuffing meats and vegetables.

PREPARATION TIME: 10 MINUTES
COOKING TIME: 9 MINUTES
PER SERVING (4): KCAL: 240; FAT: 13.3G; CARBS: 25.67G; PROTEIN: 4.99G; SUGARS: 2.97G; FIBRE: 1.8G

INGREDIENTS:

- 60 ml melted butter
- 200 g slightly stale bread, cut into small cubes
- Chopped fresh parsley for garnish

INSTRUCTIONS:

Step 1: Preheat the air fryer to 180°C.

Step 2: In a bowl, combine the bread and melted butter. Toss well.

Step 3: Add the bread to the air fryer and toast for 8 to 9 minutes while shaking the basket every 3 or 4 minutes until the bread is golden brown and crispy.

Step 4: Remove them into a bowl and toss with parsley.

Step 5: Serve warm.

9. FISH STICKS AND FRIES

Can we agree that this is one of the best British lunches ever? And if the air fryer can make them so effortlessly, I am sure you'll be making tons of it.

PREPARATION TIME: 10 MINUTES
COOKING TIME: 10 MINUTES
PER SERVING (4): KCAL: 245; FAT: 9.35G; CARBS: 32.16G; PROTEIN: 8.57G; SUGARS: 1.83G; FIBRE: 3.3G

INGRENKEDIENTS:

- 450 g frozen fries
- 4 frozen fish sticks

INSTRUCTIONS:

Step 1: Preheat the air fryer to 200°C.

Step 2: Pour the fries in the air fryer basket and mist with cooking spray. Sit an air fryer-safe trivet (with good size for your air fryer) over the fries and lay the fish sticks on top. Mist everything with cooking spray.

Step 3: Air fry for 5 more minutes, turn the fish, and shake the basket with the fries. Mist again with cooking spray and air fry for 4 to 5 more minutes or until golden brown.

Step 4: Remove the fish sticks and fries onto serving plates and enjoy with your favourite sauce.

10. HAM AND CHEESE SLIDERS

Just ham, cheese, some buns, and sesame seeds and you have a speedy and delicious lunch ready in under 7 minutes.

PREPARATION TIME: 5 MINUTES
COOKING TIME: 1 MINUTE
PER SERVING (4): KCAL: 461; FAT: 30.84G; CARBS: 32.27G; PROTEIN: 13.68G; SUGARS: 16.79G; FIBRE: 0.9G

INGREDIENTS:

- 4 slider buns
- 4 slices cheddar cheese
- 4 ham slices, each folded to fit bun size
- 1 tbsp. butter, melted
- 1 tsp. black sesame seeds

INSTRUCTIONS:

Step 1: Preheat the air fryer to 175°C.

Step 2: Slice the buns in halves width wise.

Step 3: On the bottom parts of the buns, add one slice of cheese and ham each. Cover with the top parts of the buns and brush them with butter. Sprinkle on some sesame seeds.

Step 4: Place the buns in the air fryer and warm for 1 minute or until the cheese melts.

Step 5: Arrange the sliders on a serving platter and serve.

11. HONEYED BABY CARROTS

Honeyed carrots are vibrant in colour, which make them perfect for afternoon servings. Enjoy them as a side dish with many options—meats, fish, and even more vegetables.

PREPARATION TIME: 10 MINUTES
COOKING TIME: 15 MINUTES
PER SERVING (4): KCAL: 116; FAT: 3.79G; CARBS: 20.73G; PROTEIN: 1.61G; SUGARS: 12.38G; FIBRE: 4.8G

INGRENKEDIENTS:

- 680 g baby carrots
- 1 tbsp. olive oil
- 1 tbsp. honey
- Salt and black pepper to taste

INSTRUCTIONS:

Step 1: Preheat the air fryer to 185°C.

Step 2: In a bowl, combine the carrots, olive oil, honey, salt, and black pepper. Toss the carrots well.

Step 3: Add the carrots to the air fryer and cook for 12 to 15 minutes or until they are tender.

Step 4: Remove the carrots into a bowl and serve warm.

12. LEEK AND PRAWN GRATIN

This gratin bursts with much green colour, which denotes some serious health factor going on in here. Each bite is lovely.

PREPARATION TIME: 10 MINUTES
COOKING TIME: 20 MINUTES
PER SERVING (4): KCAL: 263; FAT: 17.4G; CARBS: 13.7G; PROTEIN: 14.65G; SUGARS: 4.32G; FIBRE: 1.7G

INGREDIENTS:

- 4 medium leeks, chopped
- 250 g tiger prawns, peeled and deveined
- A knob of butter, melted
- 1 tsp. mustard powder
- 100 ml double cream
- A handful of chopped fresh parsley and coriander
- Salt and black pepper to taste

NSTRUCTIONS:

Step 1: Preheat the air fryer to 200°C.

Step 2: Heat the olive oil over medium heat on a stovetop and sauté the leeks for 5 minutes or until tender.

Step 3: In a bowl, mix the leeks, prawns, butter, mustard powder, double cream, parsley, coriander, salt, and black pepper.

Step 4: Spread the mixture in two to four small baking dishes and even out the tops.

Step 5: One after the other, bake the gratin for 5 to 10 minutes or until the prawns are pink and cooked within.

Step 6: Remove the baking dishes from the oven and let them rest for 5 minutes.

Step 7: Serve the gratin warm.

13. LEMON PEPPER SHRIMP

These shrimp pack better flavour because they use fresh lemon juice with freshly ground black pepper rather than age-old lemon pepper seasoning sitting on the shelf.

PREPARATION TIME: 10 MINUTES
COOKING TIME: 8 MINUTES
PER SERVING (4): KCAL: 332; FAT: 28.17G; CARBS: 1.75G; PROTEIN: 15.49G; SUGARS: 0.19G; FIBRE: 0.1G

INGRENKEDIENTS:

- 450 g medium raw shrimp, peeled and deveined
- 2 tbsp. lemon juice
- 120 ml olive oil
- Salt and black pepper to taste

INSTRUCTIONS:

Step 1: Preheat the air fryer to 200°C.

Step 2: In a bowl, combine the shrimp, lemon juice, olive oil, salt, and black pepper. Toss well.

Step 3: Put the shrimp in the air fryer basket and cook for 6 to 8 minutes or until the shrimp is golden brown and cooked through.

Step 4: Plate the shrimp and serve warm with pasta.

14. LEMON PEPPER WINGS

In this recipe, I extend that lemon pepper love onto some chicken wings.

PREPARATION TIME: 10 MINUTES
COOKING TIME: 20 MINUTES
PER SERVING (4): KCAL: 348; FAT: 14.8G; CARBS: 0.61G; PROTEIN: 49.88G; SUGARS: 0.15G; FIBRE: 0.1G

INGREDIENTS:

- 900 g chicken wings, separated at the joints
- ½ lemon, juiced or to taste
- 2 tbsp. olive oil
- Salt and black pepper to taste

NSTRUCTIONS:

Step 1: Preheat the air fryer to 200°C.

Step 2: In a bowl, toss the chicken wings with lemon juice, olive oil, salt, and black pepper.

Step 3: Put the wings in the air fryer basket and cook for 8 to 10 minutes per side or until they are golden brown and the chicken reaches an internal temperature of 74°C.

Step 4: Remove the wings onto a plate and let rest for 5 minutes.

Step 5: Serve the wings warm.

15. MARGHERITA PIZZA

When I discovered I could make pizza in the air fryer, I made many of them. However, one of my go-to ones for a quick lunch is the margherita pizza, which requires only four ingredients.

PREPARATION TIME: 10 MINUTES
COOKING TIME: 8 MINUTES
PER SERVING (4): KCAL: 440; FAT: 27.99G; CARBS: 20.77G; PROTEIN: 25.91G; SUGARS: 4.32G; FIBRE: 1.9G

INGRENKEDIENTS:

- 225 g pizza dough, store-bought
- 120 ml pizza sauce
- 340 g fresh mozzarella, sliced
- 4 tsp. fresh basil leaves, thinly sliced

INSTRUCTIONS:

Step 1: Preheat the air fryer to 185°C.

Step 2: Lay the pizza dough in the air fryer basket and cook for 3 minutes.

Step 3: After, spread the pizza sauce on top of the dough and distribute the mozzarella cheese and basil on top.

Step 4: Bake for 5 minutes or until the cheese melts and the pizza dough is golden brown and cooked through.

Step 5: Take out the pizza, slice, and serve.

16. ROASTED POTATO SALAD

I assume you've had creamy potato salad many times but have you had roasted potato salad? This is a no-cream version that is roasted and coated in a rich lemon oil and herb dressing, and some capers to finish off.

PREPARATION TIME: 10 MINUTES
COOKING TIME: 25 MINUTES
PER SERVING (4): KCAL: 277; FAT: 7.56G; CARBS: 49.11G; PROTEIN: 6.1G; SUGARS: 3.34G; FIBRE: 7G

INGREDIENTS:

- 1 kg new potatoes, well-scrubbed and halved
- 2 tbsp. olive oil
- Salt and black pepper to taste
- 2 tbsp. fresh lemon juice
- 1 red onion, thinly sliced
- 2 tbsp. chopped fresh parsley
- 2 tbsp. chopped fresh dill
- 2 tbsp. capers

NSTRUCTIONS:

Step 1: Preheat the air fryer to 200°C.

Step 2: In a bowl, toss the potatoes, olive oil, salt, and black pepper.

Step 3: Add the potatoes to the air fryer and cook for 20 to 25 minutes or until the potatoes are golden brown and tender.

Step 4: Remove them into a bowl and add the lemon juice, onion, parsley, dill, and capers.

Step 5: Mix them well and serve warm.

17. SAUSAGE, PEPPERS, AND ONION SUB SANDWICHES

Sub sandwiches are awesome in that you can fill them with just about anything and they should work. Here, I tried out some sausages, peppers, and onion for a natural balance of savouriness, sweetness, and intense flavours.

PREPARATION TIME: 10 MINUTES
COOKING TIME: 18 MINUTES
PER SERVING (4): KCAL: 549; FAT: 33.88G; CARBS: 36.63G; PROTEIN: 24.65G; SUGARS: 7.22G; FIBRE: 3.4G

INGREDIENTS:

- 1 tbsp. olive oil
- 4 British pork sausages, cut into chunks
- ½ medium red onion, sliced
- 1 red bell pepper, deseeded and sliced
- 1 yellow bell pepper, deseeded and sliced
- Salt and black pepper
- 4 sub rolls
- 240 ml marinara sauce
- 225 g grated mozzarella and Parmesan cheeses

INSTRUCTIONS:

Step 1: Preheat the air fryer to 175°C.

Step 2: Heat the olive oil in a skillet over medium heat on a stovetop. Add the sausages and cook for 8 to 10 minutes or until they are brown. Remove them onto a plate.

Step 3: In the skillet, add the onion and peppers, and sauté for 5 minutes or until they are tender. Season them with salt and black pepper.

Step 4: Split the rolls without cutting them all the way through to the end. Spread marinara sauce inside them on both top and bottom buns. Fill them with the sausages, peppers and onion, and cheeses.

Step 5: Place them in the air fryer and warm for 2 to 3 minutes or until the cheeses melt.

Step 6: Take them out onto plates and serve them warm.

18. SCALLOPS WITH BUTTERNUT SQUASH SAUCE

Whipping up quick butternut squash sauce with scallops is simply an effortless gourmet way of having easy scallops right at home. You can also pair this dish with polenta for a heavier serving.

PREPARATION TIME: 10 MINUTES
COOKING TIME: 28 MINUTES
PER SERVING (4): KCAL: 243; FAT: 17.93G; CARBS: 5.98G; PROTEIN: 14.75G; SUGARS: 1.41G; FIBRE: 0.6G

INGREDIENTS:

For the butternut squash:

- ½ (900 g) butternut squash, peeled, deseeded, and cubed
- 1 tbsp. olive oil
- 110 ml double cream
- Salt and black pepper

For the scallops:

- 450 g scallops
- 1 tbsp. melted butter
- 1 tsp. lemon pepper seasoning
- 1/2 tsp. paprika
- Salt and black pepper to taste (optional)

INSTRUCTIONS:

For the butternut squash sauce:

Step 1: Preheat the air fryer to 170°C.

Step 2: In a bowl, toss the butternut squash with olive oil. Add it to the air fryer and cook for 15 to 20 minutes or until just cooked but not browned.

Step 3: Remove them into a blender. Add the double cream and season with salt and black pepper. Blend until smooth.

For the scallops:

Step 4: In a bowl, toss the scallops with melted butter, lemon pepper seasoning, paprika, salt, and black pepper (if needed).

Step 5: Cook them in the air fryer at 200°C for 3 to 4 minutes per side or until golden brown and opaque.

Step 6: Drizzle some of the butternut squash sauce on serving plates and top with the scallops.

Step 7: Serve warm.

19. SEASONED RAINBOW CARROTS

On your next visit to the farmer's market, make sure to grab some fresh rainbow carrots to explore this multi-seasoning kind of a recipe.

PREPARATION TIME: 10 MINUTES
COOKING TIME: 15 MINUTES
PER SERVING (4): KCAL: 80; FAT: 3.66G; CARBS: 11.49G; PROTEIN: 1.14G; SUGARS: 5.46G; FIBRE: 3.4G

INGRENKEDIENTS:

- 450 g rainbow carrots
- 1 tbsp. olive oil
- 1 tsp. of your favourite dried mixed seasoning
- Salt and black pepper to taste (if needed)
- Fresh mint or basil leaves for garnish
- Some dry seasoning options: garden herb, Italian, piri piri, Mediterranean, Greek, 7-spice

INSTRUCTIONS:

Step 1: Preheat the air fryer to 185°C.

Step 2: In a bowl, combine the carrots, olive oil, seasoning mix, salt, and black pepper (if needed). Toss the carrots well.

Step 3: Add the carrots to the air fryer basket and cook for 12 to 15 minutes or until they are tender.

Step 4: Remove the carrots into a bowl, garnish with mint or basil, and serve warm.

20. SPAGHETTI SQUASH WITH BEEF AND CHEESE

Everything bakes in the air fryer and it is your perfect cheat out of eating regular pasta with beef and cheese.

PREPARATION TIME: 10 MINUTES
COOKING TIME: 21 MINUTES
PER SERVING (4): KCAL: 694; FAT: 45.69G; CARBS: 30.08G; PROTEIN: 43.45G; SUGARS: 9.36G; FIBRE: 4.6G

INGREDIENTS:

- 1 medium whole spaghetti squash
- 45 ml olive oil
- Salt and black pepper to taste
- 450 g beef mince
- 1 medium yellow onion, diced
- 3 garlic cloves, minced
- 1 tbsp. mixed herb seasoning
- 1/2 tsp. red pepper flakes
- 120 ml tomato pasta sauce
- 225 g ricotta cheese
- 110 g mozzarella cheese
- 85 g Parmesan cheese

NSTRUCTIONS:

Step 1: Preheat the air fryer to 200°C.

Step 2: Cut the spaghetti squash in half lengthwise, scoop out the seeds, and season the insides with 2 tbsp. of olive oil, salt, and black pepper.

Step 3: Sit the squash halves in the air fryer basket and bake for 12 to 15 minutes or until the flesh is tender.

Step 4: Meanwhile, in a skillet over medium heat on a stove top, brown the beef for 8 minutes. Add the onion, garlic, and red pepper flakes and cook for 3 minutes. Season with the mixed herbs, salt, and black pepper. Pour on the tomato sauce and cook for 4 more minutes and stir in the ricotta cheese.

Step 5: When the spaghetti squash has cooked, remove it onto a flat surface and use two forks to shred the insides to look like small strands of pasta.

Step 6: Fill the spaghetti squash with the beef mixture and then top with the mozzarella cheese and Parmesan cheese.

Step 7: Put the filled spaghetti squash in the air fryer and bake for 3 to 5 minutes or until the cheeses melt.

Step 8: Take them out and serve warm.

21. SPICY GREEN BEANS

I am sure you've had green beans many times as a side dish. How about adding some chillies this time.

PREPARATION TIME: 10 MINUTES
COOKING TIME: 10 MINUTES
PER SERVING (4): KCAL: 86; FAT: 4.88G; CARBS: 10.22G; PROTEIN: 2.65G; SUGARS: 4.91G; FIBRE: 3.4G

INGRENKEDIENTS:

- 450 g fresh green beans, trimmed and cut into thirds
- 1 tbsp. vegetable oil
- 1 tsp. sesame oil
- 1 tsp. soy sauce
- 1 tsp. rice wine vinegar
- ½ tsp. minced garlic
- 1 to 2 red hot chilli pepper, finely chopped

INSTRUCTIONS:

Step 1: Preheat the air fryer to 190°C.

Step 2: Add all the ingredients to a bowl and toss until the green beans are well-coated with the seasoning.

Step 3: Put the green beans in the air fryer basket and cook for 8 to 10 minutes or until they are tender.

Step 4: Plate the green beans and serve them warm.

22. STICKY SWEET CHICKEN BREASTS

It is truly sticky and sweet and doesn't require much effort to make. Yet the outcome is superb and with a shiny sauce to please you.

PREPARATION TIME: 10 MINUTES
COOKING TIME: 12 MINUTES
PER SERVING (4): KCAL: 660; FAT: 13.77G; CARBS: 26.82G; PROTEIN: 103.94G; SUGARS: 22.03G; FIBRE: 0.9G

INGREDIENTS:

For the chicken:

- 4 chicken breasts, skinless and boneless
- 1 tbsp. olive oil
- Salt and black pepper to taste

For the sticky sweet sauce:

- 1 tbsp. butter
- 1 tbsp. chopped garlic
- 60 ml chicken broth
- 75 ml honey
- 1 tbsp. soy sauce
- 1 tbsp. rice vinegar
- 1 tsp. red pepper flakes
- 1 tsp. black pepper

INSTRUCTIONS:

For the chicken:

Step 1: Preheat the air fryer to 200°C.

Step 2: Rub the chicken on both sides with olive oil and season with salt and black pepper.

Step 3: Put the chicken in the air fryer basket and cook for 5 to 6 minutes per side or until golden brown and reaches an internal temperature of 74°C.

For the sticky sweet sauce:

Step 4: As the chicken cooks, melt the butter in a small saucepan over medium heat on a stovetop.

Step 5: Add the garlic and sauté for 1 minute or until fragrant.

Step 6: Pour in the chicken broth, honey, soy sauce, rice vinegar, red pepper flakes, and black pepper. Boil the sauce for 2 to 4 minutes or until the sauce slightly thickens and can coat the back of your spoon.

Step 7: Brush the chicken with the sauce and cook for 1 more minute or until it feels sticky.

Step 8: Transfer the chicken to a serving platter and let them rest for 5 minutes.

Step 9: Serve warm.

23. TURKEY BREASTS WITH GRILLED PEARS

If you haven't gotten around to enjoying turkey breasts often, here's one fine reason to do so. These turkey breasts pair with deliciously grilled pears like none other. And guess what, the turkey is wrapped in bacon. You're in for a treat.

PREPARATION TIME: 10 MINUTES
COOKING TIME: 40 MINUTES
PER SERVING (4): KCAL: 2035; FAT: 93.4G; CARBS: 32.27G; PROTEIN: 252.01G; SUGARS: 20.71G; FIBRE: 6G

iNGRENKEDiENTS:

For the turkey breasts:
- 2 turkey breasts
- 1 tsp. onion powder
- 1 tsp. garlic powder
- 1 tsp. paprika
- 1 tsp. dried thyme
- Salt and black pepper to taste
- 4 bacon slices

For the grilled pears:
- 4 pears, peeled and cut in halves lengthwise
- 1 tbsp. olive oil
- 1 tbsp. honey or maple syrup

iNSTRUCTiONS:

Step 1: Preheat the air fryer to 180°C.

Step 2: Pat the turkey breasts dry with paper towels. In a bowl, mix the onion powder, garlic powder, paprika, thyme, salt, and black pepper. Season the turkey on both sides with the season and then wrap each one fully with two bacon slices each. Tuck the ends in.

Step 3: Put the wrapped turkey in the air fryer basket and bake for 20 minutes. Reduce the temperature to 150°C and bake for 10 more minutes or until the turkey reaches an internal temperature of 76°C.

Step 4: Remove the turkey onto a plate, tent them with foil, and let them rest for 10 to 15 minutes.

For the grilled pears:

Step 5: Brush the inner parts of the pears with olive oil and honey.

Step 6: Put them in the air fryer with the inner sides facing upwards and "grill" at 180°C for 10 minutes or until they are golden brown.

Step 7: Remove the pears onto a plate.

Step 8: Slice the turkey breasts and serve them with the grilled pears.

24. TURKEY MEATBALLS

These are simple meatballs that use turkey mince and then are packed with herbs. They are a fantastic topping over pasta.

PREPARATION TIME: 10 MINUTES
COOKING TIME: 15 MINUTES
PER SERVING (4): KCAL: 241; FAT: 10.49G; CARBS: 10.78G; PROTEIN: 25.68G; SUGARS: 0.92G; FIBRE: 0.9G

iNGREDiENTS:

- 450 g turkey mince
- 2 garlic cloves, minced
- 110 g breadcrumbs
- 1 tsp. dried oregano
- 2 tbsp. chopped fresh parsley
- Salt and black pepper to taste
- 1 egg, lightly beaten

iNSTRUCTiONS:

Step 1: Preheat the air fryer to 180°C.

Step 2: Combine all the ingredients in a bowl and mix well. After, form 8 meatballs from the mixture.

Step 3: Mist the air fryer basket with cooking spray, add the meatballs, and mist their tops with cooking spray.

Step 4: Air fry the meatballs for 4 minutes per side or until they are golden brown and have reached an internal temperature of 76°C.

Step 5: Remove the turkey meatballs onto a serving platter and let rest for 10 to 15 minutes before serving.

25. WATER CHESTNUT AND TUNA FISH CAKES

By simply introducing water chestnut to what would have been a standard tuna fish cake recipe, you get a merge of sweetness, tartness, and nuttiness all packed with the savoury flavour of tuna. Now, that is enriching.

PREPARATION TIME: 10 MINUTES
COOKING TIME: 12 MINUTES
PER SERVING (4): KCAL: 395; FAT: 15.1G; CARBS: 25.72G; PROTEIN: 39.18G; SUGARS: 3.27G; FIBRE: 1.1G

INGREDIENTS:

- 2 (340 g) cans of chunk tuna in water, drained
- 1 (140 g) can water chestnuts in water, drained and chopped
- ½ diced white onion
- 60 ml mayonnaise
- 2 eggs, lightly beaten
- 110 g seasoned breadcrumbs
- 2 tbsp. fresh lemon juice
- Salt and black pepper to taste
- Lemon wedges for serving

INSTRUCTIONS:

Step 1: Preheat the air fryer to 190°C.

Step 2: In a bowl, add the tuna, chestnuts, white onion, mayonnaise, eggs, breadcrumbs, lemon juice, salt, and black pepper. Mix well and form four patties from the mixture. Put the patties in the fridge for 20 minutes.

Step 3: Mist the air fryer with cooking spray, put the fish cakes in it, and mist the tops with cooking spray.

Step 4: Air fry for 6 minutes or until golden brown and compacted.

Step 5: Plate the tuna fish cakes and serve warm with lemon wedges.

SECTION 5.

DINNER

**Don't Forget To Get The Color Images FREE!
Simply Scan The QR Code Below!**

Please scan the QR code below to access your bonus PDF with all 150 recipes with full coloured photos & beautiful designs alongside!

This is the only way we can get the recipes with coloured photos to you & keep the book as reasonably priced as possible.

Also, once downloaded you can take the PDF with you digitally wherever you go- meaning you can cook these recipes wherever you may be! (As long as you have an air fryer!)

We hope you enjoy and do let us know your feedback!

(INSERT QR CODE HERE)

STEP BY STEP Guide-
1. Open Your Phones (Or Any Device You Want The Book On) Back Camera. The Back Camera Is The One You use as if you are taking a picture of someone.
2. Simply point your Camera at the QR code and 'tap' the QR code with your finger to focus the camera.
3. A link / pop up will appear. Simply tap that (and make sure you have internet connection) and the FREE PDF containing all of the coloured images should appear.
4. Now you have access to these FOREVER. Simply 'Bookmark' The tab it opened on, or download the document and take wherever you want.
5. Repeat this on any device you want it on! (If you want it on a laptop, simply email the document to yourself!)

Any issues please email us at **vicandersonpublishing@gmail.com** and we will be happy to help!!

1. BAKED STUFFED AUBERGINE

On some days, I serve these stuffed aubergine as they are because they are well stuffed. On other days, I like to have them with some lamb and it is just a mouthful of goodness.

PREPARATION TIME: 10 MINUTES
COOKING TIME: 15 MINUTES
PER SERVING (4): KCAL: 296; FAT: 19.42G; CARBS: 23.03G; PROTEIN: 2.45G; SUGARS: 12.98G; FIBRE: 11.1G

INGRENKEDIENTS:

- 2 medium aubergines
- 1 tbsp. olive oil
- Salt and black pepper to taste
- ½ tsp. dried thyme
- 680 g cherry tomatoes, quartered
- 1 garlic clove, minced
- 90 ml tahini sauce
- 225 g grated mozzarella cheese
- Chopped fresh parsley for garnish

INSTRUCTIONS:

Step 1: Preheat the air fryer to 180°C.

Step 2: Cut the aubergines in halves lengthwise and, using a knife, score the flesh of the aubergine without cutting through the skin of the aubergine. Drizzle the aubergines with 1 tbsp. of olive oil and season with salt, black pepper, and thyme.

Step 3: Put the aubergines in the air fryer basket and bake for 8 to 10 minutes or until the aubergines are tender.

Step 4: Remove the aubergines onto a plate, let cool slightly, and scoop the flesh into a bowl. Add the tomatoes, the remaining olive oil, garlic, tahini sauce, salt, and black pepper. Mix well and spoon the tomato mixture into the aubergine skin. Top with the cheese.

Step 5: Place the aubergines in the air fryer and bake for 3 to 5 minutes or until the cheese melts.

Step 6: Remove the aubergines onto a plate and garnish with parsley.

Step 7: Serve warm.

2. BEEF AND VEGETABLE MEATLOAF

I pack this meatloaf with some yellow peppers, onion, and carrots to create a unison of colour, certify its healthiness, and make it better flavoured.

PREPARATION TIME: 10 MINUTES
COOKING TIME: 21 MINUTES
PER SERVING (4): KCAL: 540; FAT: 25.84G; CARBS: 37.74G; PROTEIN: 40.69G; SUGARS: 13.19G; FIBRE: 2.5G

INGREDIENTS:

- 680 g beef mince
- 160 ml milk
- 225 g breadcrumbs
- 1 large egg, cracked into a bowl
- ½ medium onion, chopped
- 1 small yellow bell pepper, deseeded and chopped
- 1 carrot, finely grated
- 1 garlic clove, minced
- Salt and black pepper to taste
- 120 ml ketchup
- 1 tsp. Worcestershire Sauce
- 1 tsp. mustard
- 30 g brown sugar

NSTRUCTIONS:

Step 1: Preheat the air fryer to 190°C.

Step 2: In a bowl, mix the beef, milk, breadcrumbs, egg, onion, bell pepper, carrot, garlic, salt, and black pepper.

Step 3: Grease a loaf pan (good size for your air fryer) with cooking spray. Spread the beef mixture in it.

Step 4: Place the loaf pan in the air fryer and bake for 16 to 18 minutes.

Step 5: In a bowl, mix the ketchup, Worcestershire sauce, mustard, and brown sugar until smooth. Spread the sauce over the meatloaf.

Step 6: When the air fryer's timer is done, open it and spread the sauce on the meatloaf. Bake for 2 to 3 more minutes or until it is sticky.

Step 7: Remove the loaf pan and let it rest for 10 minutes.

Step 8: Run a butter knife along the edges of the meatloaf and transfer it to a plate. Slice and serve warm.

The UK Air Fryer Cookbook for Beginners

3. BEETS, ONIONS, AND LEEKS

At first sight, this rich red play on vegetables will woo you in. And when you have a bite, I believe it'll be one of your favourite dinner sides.

PREPARATION TIME: 10 MINUTES
COOKING TIME: 20 MINUTES
PER SERVING (4): KCAL: 78; FAT: 3.57 G; CARBS: 10.99G; PROTEIN: 1.48G; SUGARS: 5.23G; FIBRE: 2.4G

INGRENKEDIENTS:

- 2 beets, peeled and cut into chunks
- 1 leek, chopped
- 1 large white onion, cut into chunks
- 1 tbsp. olive oil
- 1 tsp. dried thyme
- Salt and black pepper to taste

INSTRUCTIONS:

Step 1: Preheat the air fryer to 200°C.

Step 2: In a bowl, add the beets, leek, onion, olive oil, thyme, salt, and black pepper. Toss well.

Step 3: Add the vegetables to the air fryer and roast for 15 to 20 minutes or until they are tender. Meanwhile, shake the basket every 5 minutes during cooking.

Step 4: Spoon the vegetables onto a plate and serve warm.

4. BONE-IN PORK CHOPS WITH BREADING

On those days when you can't be fancy about dinner, this quickly breaded pork chops recipe will come in handy. Pair it with roasted vegetables and you can call it an evening.

PREPARATION TIME: 10 MINUTES
COOKING TIME: 12 MINUTES
PER SERVING (4): KCAL: 407; FAT: 11.94G; CARBS: 20.97G; PROTEIN: 50.37G; SUGARS: 0.77G; FIBRE: 1.1G

INGREDIENTS:

- 4 pork chops, boneless
- 110 g plain flour
- 1 tsp. garlic powder
- 1 tsp. onion powder
- 2 large eggs
- 1 tsp. water
- 75 g seasoned breadcrumbs
- 75 g grated Parmesan cheese
- Chopped fresh parsley for garnish
- Salt and black pepper to taste

INSTRUCTIONS:

Step 1: Preheat the air fryer to 200°C.

Step 2: Pat dry the pork with paper towels and season with salt and black pepper.

Step 3: On a plate, mix the flour and half of each of the garlic powder, and onion powder. Crack the eggs into a bowl and whisk with the water. On another plate, mix the breadcrumbs, remaining garlic and onion powders, and Parmesan cheese.

Step 4: Dredge the pork chops on both sides in the flour, then dip in the eggs, and then coat well with the breadcrumb mixture.

Step 5: Mist the air fryer basket with cooking spray, lay in the pork chops, and mist their tops with cooking spray.

Step 6: Bake for 5 to 6 minutes per side or until the pork chops are golden brown and reach an internal temperature of 63°C.

Step 7: Plate the pork chops and let them rest for 10 minutes before serving.

5. BROCCOLI PARMESAN

Parmesan improves the look and flavour of broccoli and sometimes I like to go extra on my Parmesan sprinkle.

PREPARATION TIME: 10 MINUTES
COOKING TIME: 10 MINUTES
PER SERVING (4): KCAL: 96; FAT: 8.58G; CARBS: 2.94G; PROTEIN: 2.55G; SUGARS: 0.41G; FIBRE: 0.7G

INGRENKEDIENTS:

- 2 tbsp. olive oil
- 1 tsp. garlic powder
- 60 g grated Parmesan cheese + extra for topping
- 1 small head of broccoli, chopped into florets

INSTRUCTIONS:

Step 1: Preheat the air fryer to 180°C.

Step 2: In a bowl, mix the olive oil, garlic powder, and Parmesan cheese. Add the broccoli and toss well.

Step 3: Add the broccoli to the air fryer basket and bake for 8 to 10 minutes or until fork tender.

Step 4: Remove the broccoli into a bowl and sprinkle with more Parmesan cheese.

Step 5: Serve warm.

6. COTTAGE PIE

Just like grandma would make it, this cottage pie packs all the essentials. I'll teach you how to make it with the air fryer.

PREPARATION TIME: 10 MINUTES
COOKING TIME: 16 MINUTES
PER SERVING (4): KCAL: 403; FAT: 20.56G; CARBS: 29.92G; PROTEIN: 25.65G; SUGARS: 1.76G; FIBRE: 4.8G

INGREDIENTS:

- 450 g chicken or turkey mince
- 1 (340 g) jar chicken gravy
- ½ tsp. onion powder
- 335 g frozen mixed vegetables, thawed and drained
- Salt and black pepper to taste
- 450 g mashed potatoes
- 2 tbsp. butter, melted

NSTRUCTIONS:

Step 1: Preheat the air fryer to 180°C.

Step 2: In a pot, add the chicken or turkey and cook for 6 minutes over medium heat on a stovetop or until no longer pink. Season with salt and black pepper.

Step 3: Pour in the gravy and stir in the onion powder and mixed vegetables. Cook for 3 more minutes.

Step 4: Spoon the sauce into a baking dish (with good size for your air fryer). In a bowl, mix the mashed potatoes and melted butter. Spoon and spread the mashed potatoes on the sauce.

Step 4: Place the baking dish in the air fryer and bake for 5 to 7 minutes or until golden brown on top.

Step 5: Remove the baking dish, let cool for 3 to 5 minutes, and serve.

7. GARLIC BUTTER SALMON

I had the best garlic butter salmon and when I asked how it was made, I learned it contained only five everyday ingredients. So, I tried it out with my air fryer and it was completely no fuss. Here is the same winning recipe.

PREPARATION TIME: 10 MINUTES
COOKING TIME: 10 MINUTES
PER SERVING (4): KCAL: 509; FAT: 25.53G; CARBS: 0.66G; PROTEIN: 65.43G; SUGARS: 0.02G; FIBRE: 0.1G

INGREDIENTS:

- 4 salmon fillets, skin-on
- 60 g butter, melted
- 2 tsp. minced garlic
- Salt and black pepper to taste

INSTRUCTIONS:

Step 1: Preheat the air fryer to 180°C.

Step 2: Pat dry the salmon fillets. In a bowl, mix the butter, garlic, salt, and black pepper. Brush the salmon on both sides with the mixture.

Step 3: Lay the salmon fillets in the air fryer basket with the skin side down and bake for 8 to 10 minutes or until golden brown and flaky.

Step 4: Remove the salmon onto a plate and let rest for 3 to 5 minutes.

Step 5: Serve warm.

8. HERBED POTATOES STUFFED WHOLE CHICKEN

The science behind stuffing potatoes into whole chicken is quite reversed. You might think the herbed potatoes help season the chicken. Although they do, the chicken rather packs more flavour into the potatoes when they are done. It makes them juicier too.

PREPARATION TIME: 15 MINUTES
COOKING TIME: 1 HOUR 24 MINUTES
PER SERVING (4): KCAL: 1031; FAT: 40.84G; CARBS: 93.47G; PROTEIN: 73.28G; SUGARS: 8.37G; FIBRE: 10.1G

INGREDIENTS:

- 6 medium red potatoes, peeled and cut into 1-inch cubes
- 450 g Italian sausage links, casings removed
- 1 tbsp. butter
- 225 g finely chopped onion
- 2 tsp. dried thyme
- 4 tsp. dried parsley
- 1 tsp. dried rosemary, crushed
- Salt and black pepper to taste
- 1 (3.5 kg) roasting chicken, cavity removed and well-cleaned
- 1 tbsp. canola oil
- 240 ml water

INSTRUCTIONS:

Step 1: Preheat the air fryer to 180°C.

Step 2: Boil the potatoes in slightly salted water for 10 to 15 minutes or until they are tender. Drain them.

Step 3: Cook the sausage in a non-stick skillet over medium heat on a stovetop for 5 minutes. Spoon the sausage onto a plate and set it aside.

Step 4: Melt the butter in the same skillet and sauté the onion for 3 minutes or until tender. Stir in the potatoes, thyme, parsley, rosemary, salt, and black pepper. Cook for 1 minute and stir in the sausage. Turn the heat off.

Step 5: Rub the chicken all around and all corners with canola oil and season with salt and black pepper.

Step 6. Spoon the potato mixture into the cavity and then tie the chicken legs together using butcher's twine.

Step 7: Place the chicken in the air fryer and bake for 30 minutes. Turn the chicken over and bake for 30 more minutes or until golden brown and it reaches an internal temperature of 74°C.

Step 8: Remove the chicken onto a chopping board and let rest for 10 to 15 minutes before slicing and serving.

9. HOT GAME PIE

I wasn't a big lover of game meat while growing up but now I love it in pies. This one is served hot from the air fryer while the gamey flavours are still fresh and the sauce is bubbly.

PREPARATION TIME: 15 MINUTES
COOKING TIME: 63 MINUTES
PER SERVING (4): KCAL: 982; FAT: 55.18G; CARBS: 67.08G; PROTEIN: 43.79G; SUGARS: 6.31G; FIBRE: 4.1G

INGRENKEDIENTS:

- 500 g of your preferred game, diced
- Salt and black pepper to taste
- 45 ml olive oil
- 4 bacon slices, cut into 2 cm pieces
- 300 g mushrooms, cut into bite-sized chunks
- 2 large red onions, thinly sliced
- 2 garlic cloves, minced
- 30 g plain white flour, plus more if needed
- 480 ml chicken or vegetable stock
- 240 ml red wine
- 2 bay leaves
- 2 sprigs of fresh thyme or rosemary
- 1 (400 g) refrigerated package pie crust, defrosted
- 1 egg, beaten

INSTRUCTIONS:

Step 1: Season the game with salt and black pepper. Heat 2 tbsp. of olive oil in a skillet over medium heat and sear the game on both sides for about 10 minutes or until brown. Spoon the game onto a plate.

Step 2: Cook the bacon in the skillet for 5 minutes or until golden brown. Spoon it to the side of the game.

Step 3: Heat the remaining olive oil in the skillet and sauté the mushrooms for 10 minutes or until it has lost most of its liquid. Stir in the onions and sauté for 3 minutes or until tender. Stir in the garlic and cook for 1 minute or until fragrant.

Step 4: Mix in the flour and cook for 1 minute and add the stock, red wine, bay leaves, and thyme or rosemary. Let come to a boil and return the game and bacon to the pot. Simmer for 10 to 15 minutes or until sauce thickens slightly and the game cooks through.

Step 5: Preheat the air fryer to 180°C.

Step 6: Spoon the sauce into a pie dish (with a good size for your air fryer) and cover the dish with the puff pastry. Crimp the edges to seal, trim off any excess, and brush the top with eggs. Also, use a knife to cut 1 to 3 slits through the pastry.

Step 7: Place the dish in the air fryer and bake for 15 to 18 minutes or until the crust is golden brown and the filling is bubbly.

Step 8: Remove the dish from the air fryer, let it rest for 2 minutes, and serve hot.

10. LAMB AND SPRING VEGETABLES

It is a straightforward lamb dish with colourful roasted vegetables that is perfect for the family.

PREPARATION TIME: 15 MINUTES
COOKING TIME: 60 MINUTES
PER SERVING (4): KCAL: 819; FAT: 43.26G; CARBS: 6.24G; PROTEIN: 95.57G; SUGARS: 3.09G; FIBRE: 1.8G

INGREDIENTS:

- 1.4 kg leg of lamb roast
- 2 tbsp. olive oil
- Salt and black pepper to taste
- 1/2 tsp. thyme, dried
- 1 tsp. rosemary, dried
- ½ bunch green onions
- 225 g medium carrots
- 225 g green beans, trimmed
- 1 large red chilli
- 2 garlic cloves, crushed and peeled
- 3 fresh rosemary sprigs
- 3 fresh thyme sprigs

NSTRUCTIONS:

Step 1: Preheat the air fryer to 200°C.

Step 2: Pat dry the lamb with paper towels. In a bowl, mix 1 tbsp. of olive oil, salt, black pepper, thyme, and rosemary. Rub the seasoning all over the lamb.

Step 3: In a bowl, toss the green onions, carrots, green beans, and red chilli with the remaining olive oil, salt, and black pepper.

Step 4: Sit the lamb in the air fryer basket and distribute the vegetables around it. Stick the garlic, rosemary, and thyme sprigs around the lamb.

Step 5: Close the air fryer and roast for 50 to 60 minutes or until the lamb is golden brown and reaches an internal temperature of 63°C. Meanwhile, turn the lamb halfway through cooking.

Step 6: Remove the lamb and vegetables onto a platter, tent the lamb with foil and let it rest for 10 to 15 minutes before slicing.

Step 7: Serve the lamb with the vegetables.

11. MAPLE AND MUSTARD GLAZED HAM

I keep the recipe standard here and only share some accuracy for how you can make it with the air fryer. The goal is to keep the aromas and tastes as traditional as should be.

PREPARATION TIME: 10 MINUTES
COOKING TIME: 40 MINUTES
PER SERVING (4): KCAL: 1201; FAT: 28.66G; CARBS: 106.97G; PROTEIN: 123.76G; SUGARS: 101.01G; FIBRE: 0.02G

INGRENKEDIENTS:

- 240 ml maple syrup
- 1 tbsp. Dijon mustard
- 225 g packed light brown sugar
- 1 (2.5 kg) boneless half ham, fully cooked

INSTRUCTIONS:

Step 1: Preheat the air fryer to 150°C.

Step 2: In a small saucepan, combine the maple syrup, brown sugar, and Dijon mustard. Stir and cook over low heat on a stovetop for 2 to 3 minutes or until the sugar dissolves.

Step 3: Line the air fryer with foil and place the ham in it. Spoon half of the maple glaze over the ham.

Step 4: Bake for 35 to 40 minutes or until golden brown.

Step 5: Remove the ham onto a chopping board and brush the remaining maple syrup all over it.

Step 6: Slice and serve warm.

12. MARINATED BARBECUE LAMB

Making this at home will be a real treat. Grab your favourite barbecue seasoning and sauce, and start making some delicious food.

PREPARATION TIME: 40 MINUTES
COOKING TIME: 10 MINUTES
PER SERVING (4): KCAL: 246; FAT: 10.11G; CARBS: 28.85G; PROTEIN: 0.05G; SUGARS: 23.85G; FIBRE: 0.9G

INGREDIENTS:

- 4 lamb chops
- 2 tbsp. olive oil
- 1 tsp. barbecue seasoning
- 1/2 tsp. dried oregano
- Salt and black pepper to taste
- 240 ml barbecue sauce

NSTRUCTIONS:

Step 1: Pat dry the lamb and place them in a zipper bag. In a bowl, mix the olive oil, barbecue seasoning, oregano, salt, and black pepper. Pour on the seasoning, zip the bag, and rub the seasoning on the lamb. Let the lamb marinate in the fridge for 30 minutes.

Step 2: Preheat the air fryer to 200°C.

Step 3: Place the lamb in the air fryer basket and cook for 3 to 4 minutes per side. Brush the lamb with the barbecue sauce and cook for 1 to 2 more minutes.

Step 4: Remove the lamb chops onto a plate and let them rest for 10 minutes.

Step 5: Serve warm.

13. PORK AND HAM PIE

This century-long recipe has stayed intact until date and now we can make the pie crust even crunchier. I believe that's the goal for making it in the air fryer, besides its quicker cooking time.

PREPARATION TIME: 10 MINUTES
COOKING TIME: 33 MINUTES
PER SERVING (4): KCAL: 1561; FAT: 104.13G; CARBS: 103.92G; PROTEIN: 50.5G; SUGARS: 1.01G; FIBRE: 4.2G

INGRENKEDIENTS:

- 400 g pork mince
- 200 g pork sausage meat
- 140 g cooked ham meat, chopped into small chunks
- 1 small onion, finely chopped
- A small handful of sage, chopped
- Salt and black pepper to taste
- 2 to 3 shakes of hot sauce
- 4 hard-boiled eggs, shells removed
- 2 (400 g) refrigerated package pie crusts, defrosted
- 1 egg, beaten

INSTRUCTIONS:

Step 1: In a skillet on a stovetop, brown the pork mince and pork sausage meat for 10 minutes or until brown. Add the ham meat and cook for 2 minutes. Stir in the onion and sage, and cook for 3 to 5 minutes. Season well with the salt, black pepper, and hot sauce to your taste.

Step 2: Preheat the air fryer to 180°C.

Step 3: Grease four medium ramekins with cooking spray and line them with one pie crust to slightly overlap the rims of the ramekins. Trim off the excess.

Step 4: Divide half of the pork mixture into the lined ramekins and use the back of your spoon to press them in. Place one egg onto each and fill with the remaining pork mixture. Gently press the meat over the eggs and cover the tops with pastry. Crimp the top pastry with the overlapping pieces of the bottom of the pastry. Brush their tops with the beaten egg and cut a slit on top of each pastry.

Step 5: Place the ramekins in the air fryer and bake for 15 to 18 minutes or until the crust is golden brown.

Step 6: Remove the ramekins from the air fryer and let cool slightly.

Step 7: Invert the pies out of the pastry and turn them over to stand. Serve them warm.

14. PORK BELLY ROAST

Make this super crunchy pork belly for batch-cooking. I love to serve some slices straight from the air fryer with potatoes and carrots. Then, I chop any extras and refrigerate them for future salads.

PREPARATION TIME: 15 MINUTES
COOKING TIME: 40 MINUTES
PER SERVING (4): KCAL: 941; FAT: 96.92G; CARBS: 0G; PROTEIN: 15.89G; SUGARS: 0G; FIBRE: 0G

INGREDIENTS:

- 680 g pork belly
- 2 tbsp. olive oil
- 1 tbsp. salt

INSTRUCTIONS:

Step 1: Preheat the air fryer to 160°C.

Step 2: Using a sharp knife, score the top of the pork belly and rub the top with 1 tbsp. of olive oil and season this part with salt. In a bowl, mix the remaining olive oil and salt, and rub over the parts of the pork belly.

Step 3: Place the pork belly in the air fryer and roast for 30 minutes. Increase the temperature to 195°C and roast for 5 to 10 more minutes or until the top of the pork is golden brown and crackling.

Step 4: Remove the pork belly onto a chopping board and let it rest for 10 to 15 minutes.

Step 5: Slice and serve warm.

15. PORK CHOPS WITH GRILLED PEACHES

If you haven't tried pork chops with grilled peaches, then you are in for a real treat. Savouriness and sweetness merge so awesomely here.

PREPARATION TIME: 10 MINUTES
COOKING TIME: 22 MINUTES
PER SERVING (4): KCAL: 335; FAT: 10.47G; CARBS: 19.41G; PROTEIN: 40.85G; SUGARS: 15.73G; FIBRE: 2.8G

INGRENKEDIENTS:

For the pork chops:

- 4 pork chops
- 1 tsp. onion powder
- 1 tsp. garlic powder
- 1 tsp. paprika
- 1 tsp. dried rosemary
- Salt and black pepper to taste

For the grilled peaches:

- 4 peaches, halved, stoned, and cut into wedges
- 1 tbsp. olive oil
- 1 tbsp. honey or maple syrup

INSTRUCTIONS:

Step 1: Preheat the air fryer to 200°C.

Step 2: Pat the pork chops dry with paper towels. In a bowl, mix the onion powder, garlic powder, paprika, rosemary, salt, and black pepper. Season the pork chops on both sides with the seasoning.

Step 3: Place the pork chops in the air fryer basket and bake for 6 minutes per side or until it is golden brown and reaches an internal temperature of 63°C.

Step 4: Remove the pork chops onto a plate and let it rest for 10 minutes.

For the grilled peaches:

Step 5: As the pork rests, grill the peaches.

Step 6: In a bowl, toss the peaches with olive oil and honey.

Step 7: "Grill" the peaches in the air fryer at 180°C for 10 minutes or until they are golden brown.

Step 8: Remove the pears onto a plate and serve them with the pork chops.

16. RACK OF LAMB WITH WARM SALAD

It is a simple thyme-flavoured rack of lamb but paired with delicious chunks of warmed vegetables served on a spinach bed. You can toss the salad with cooked quinoa or barley for improved texture.

PREPARATION TIME: 15 MINUTES
COOKING TIME: 35 MINUTES
PER SERVING (4): KCAL: 538; FAT: 22.86G; CARBS: 60.08G; PROTEIN: 31.77G; SUGARS: 15.92G; FIBRE: 13.5G

INGREDIENTS:

For the rack of lamb:

- 1 tbsp. olive oil
- 1 tsp. dried thyme
- 1 tsp. dried rosemary
- Salt and black pepper to taste
- 400 g lamb rack

For the warm salad:

- 1 (900 g) butternut squash, peeled and cut into 2 cm pieces
- 2 medium carrots, peeled and cut into 2 cm pieces
- 3 medium parsnips, peeled and cut into 2 cm pieces
- 1 medium red onion, peeled and cut into chunks
- 5 garlic cloves, peeled and smashed
- 1 tsp. olive oil
- Salt and black pepper to taste
- 680 g baby spinach
- 60 g chopped almonds
- 60 g pumpkin seeds
- 240 ml plain yoghurt
- 2 tbsp. fresh lemon juice
- 2 tbsp. chopped fresh dill

INSTRUCTIONS:

For the rack of lamb:

Step 1: Preheat the air fryer to 180°C.

Step 2: In a bowl, mix the olive oil, thyme, rosemary, salt, and black pepper. Rub the seasoning all over the lamb.

Step 3: Place the lamb in the air fryer basket and air fry for 15 to 20 minutes for medium doneness.

Step 4: Remove the lamb onto a chopping board, tent with foil, and let rest for 10 minutes before slicing.

For the warm salad:

Step 5: In a bowl, combine the butternut squash, carrots, parsnips, red onion, olive oil, salt, and black pepper. Toss well.

Step 6: Add the vegetables to the air fryer and roast for 10 to 15 minutes or until tender while shaking the basket halfway through cooking.

Step 7: In a bowl, combine the spinach, almonds, pumpkin seeds, and warm vegetables. In another bowl, mix the yoghurt, lemon juice, and dill. Drizzle the yoghurt dressing on the salad and toss well.

Step 8: Serve the lamb with the warm salad.

17. ROAST BEEF WITH ROSEMARY AND PARSLEY SAUCE

The power is the sauce in this case. Rosemary, parsley, garlic, and red chilli flakes combine to create a banging sauce that makes the beef taste incredible.

PREPARATION TIME: 15 MINUTES
COOKING TIME: 20 MINUTES
PER SERVING (4): KCAL: 462; FAT: 29.98G; CARBS: 2.97G; PROTEIN: 46.87G; SUGARS: 0.46G; FIBRE: 0.9G

INGRENKEDIENTS:

For the roast beef:
- 1 tbsp. olive oil
- 1 tsp. salt
- 1 tsp. dried thyme
- 1 tsp. dried rosemary
- 900 g beef roast

For the rosemary and parsley sauce:
- 225 g chopped fresh parsley
- 2 tbsp. fresh rosemary leaves, chopped
- 2 small garlic cloves, minced
- 1 lemon, juiced
- 60 ml olive oil
- Salt and black pepper to taste
- A pinch of red chilli flakes to taste

INSTRUCTIONS:

For the rack of lamb:

Step 1: Preheat the air fryer to 200°C.

Step 2: In a bowl, mix the olive oil, salt, thyme, and rosemary. Rub the seasoning all over the lamb.

Step 3: Place the beef in the air fryer basket and air fry for 15 to 20 minutes or until the beef reaches an internal temperature of 63°C.

Step 4: Remove the beef onto a chopping board, tent with foil, and let rest for 10 minutes before slicing.

For the rosemary and parsley sauce:

Step 5: In a bowl, mix all the sauce's ingredients.

Step 6: Serve the beef with the sauce.

18. SALMON WITH SESAME MUSTARD DRESSING

For a change in the way you've enjoyed salmon in the past, sesame oil brings on a unique punch via the dressing.

PREPARATION TIME: 10 MINUTES
COOKING TIME: 10 MINUTES
PER SERVING (4): KCAL: 636; FAT: 35.72G; CARBS: 9.95G; PROTEIN: 65.96G; SUGARS: 8.74G; FIBRE: 0.7G

INGREDIENTS:

For the salmon:
- 4 salmon fillets
- 1 tbsp. olive oil
- Salt and black pepper

For the sesame mustard dressing:
- 60 ml olive oil
- 1 tbsp. sesame oil
- 2 tbsp. honey
- 2 tbsp. yellow mustard
- 1 tsp. minced garlic
- 45 ml apple cider vinegar
- 1 tbsp. sesame seeds
- Salt and black pepper to taste

NSTRUCTIONS:

For the salmon:

Step 1: Preheat the air fryer to 190°C.

Step 2: Rub the olive oil on the salmon and season with salt and black pepper.

Step 3: Put the salmon in the air fryer with the skin side down and cook for 8 to 10 minutes or until the salmon is flaky.

For the sesame mustard dressing:

Step 4: In a bowl, mix all the dressing's ingredients.

Step 5: Plate the salmon when ready and drizzle the dressing on top. Serve warm.

The UK Air Fryer Cookbook for Beginners

19. SEA BASS WITH CITRUS-DRESSED BARLEY

The focus is rather on the citrus-dressed barley than the sea bass in an unusual way. White fish fillets are often best cooked with minimal seasoning. So, to enjoy a punch in flavour, we load up barley salad with amazing citrus flavours.

PREPARATION TIME: 15 MINUTES
COOKING TIME: 10 MINUTES
PER SERVING (4): KCAL: 307; FAT: 13.71G; CARBS: 17.43G; PROTEIN: 28.34G; SUGARS: 2.84G; FIBRE: 2.7G

INGREDIENTS:

For the sea bass:
- 4 sea bass fillets
- 1 tbsp. olive oil
- Salt and black pepper

For the citrus dressed barley:
- 225 g cooked barley
- 225 g cherry tomatoes, quartered
- ½ red bell pepper, deseeded and diced
- ½ yellow bell pepper, deseeded and diced
- 1 shallot, sliced
- 1 garlic clove, minced
- 60 g chopped fresh parsley
- 120 g crumbled feta cheese
- ½ lemon, zested and juiced
- 1 tbsp. olive oil
- Salt and black pepper to taste

INSTRUCTIONS:

For the salmon:

Step 1: Preheat the air fryer to 190°C.

Step 2: Brush the olive oil on the sea bass and season with salt and black pepper.

Step 3: Lay the fish in the air fryer and cook for 8 to 10 minutes or until they are flaky.

For the citrus dressed barley:

Step 4: Meanwhile, prepare the salad while the fish cooks. In a bowl, combine the barley, tomatoes, bell peppers, shallot, garlic, parsley, feta cheese, and lemon zest.

Step 5: In a small bowl, mix the lemon juice, olive oil, salt, and black pepper. Drizzle the dressing over the salad and mix well.

Step 6: Serve the ready sea bass with the barley salad.

20. STICKY SMOKED RIBS

There are many ways to make sticky smoked ribs, but I like a straightforward one that doesn't require cooking the sauce on a stovetop before basting. Here's a quick fix for you.

PREPARATION TIME: 15 MINUTES
COOKING TIME: 25 MINUTES
PER SERVING (4): KCAL: 551; FAT: 38.2G; CARBS: 7.35G; PROTEIN: 45.72G; SUGARS: 5.36G; FIBRE: 0.6G

INGREDIENTS:

For the ribs:
- 1 (900 g) baby back ribs, separated, at room temperature
- 2 tsp. olive oil
- Salt and black pepper

For the glaze:
- 1 tbsp. honey
- 2 tbsp. soy sauce
- 1 tbsp. ketchup
- 1 tbsp. yellow mustard
- 1/2 tsp. sweet paprika powder
- 1/2 tsp. smoked paprika powder
- A pinch of chilli powder

INSTRUCTIONS:

Step 1: Preheat the air fryer to 200°C.

Step 2: Rub the ribs with the olive oil and season with salt and black pepper.

Step 3: Put the ribs in the air fryer basket and cook for 12 minutes. Turn them and cook for 8 more minutes.

For the glaze:

Step 4: In a bowl, mix the honey, soy sauce, ketchup, mustard, both types of paprika, and chilli powder.

Step 5: Brush the ribs on both sides with the glaze and cook for 5 more minutes or until they are cooked through, sticky, and shiny.

21. SWEET AND SPICY BRUSSELS SPROUTS

Just another delicious recipe that chooses not to serve plain Brussels sprouts but packs them with some spice and sweetness for better taste.

PREPARATION TIME: 5 MINUTES
COOKING TIME: 15 MINUTES
PER SERVING (4): KCAL: 505; FAT: 21.87G; CARBS: 75.32G; PROTEIN: 15.64G; SUGARS: 44.49G; FIBRE: 17.4G

INGRENKEDIENTS:

- 450 g Brussels sprouts, each halved
- 2 tbsp. vegetable oil
- 2 tbsp. honey
- 1 tbsp. hot sauce
- 1/2 tsp. salt

INSTRUCTIONS:

Step 1: Preheat the air fryer to 180°C.

Step 2: Add the Brussels sprouts to a bowl.

Step 3: In a bowl, mix the vegetable oil, honey, hot sauce, and salt. Drizzle the mixture over the Brussels sprouts and toss well.

Step 4: Add the Brussels sprouts to the air fryer basket and cook for 10 to 15 minutes or until the Brussel sprouts are golden brown and tender.

Step 5: Spoon them into a bowl and serve warm.

22. THYME TURKEY LEGS

Turkey legs are perfect for the festive season as they are gamier in flavour. Hence, when cooking them, using minimal seasoning helps unveil its natural aromas best. And that's what's done here.

PREPARATION TIME: 5 MINUTES
COOKING TIME: 36 MINUTES
PER SERVING (4): KCAL: 871; FAT: 55.36G; CARBS: 6.18G; PROTEIN: 83.38G; SUGARS: 0.17G; FIBRE: 1.3G

INGREDIENTS:

- 4 turkey legs
- 2 tbsp. olive oil
- Salt and black pepper to taste
- 2 tsp. garlic powder
- 1 tsp. dried thyme

NSTRUCTIONS:

Step 1: Preheat the air fryer to 190°C.

Step 2: Drizzle the turkey legs with olive oil and season with salt, black pepper, garlic powder, and thyme.

Step 3: Put the turkey legs in the air fryer basket and air fry for 15 to 18 minutes per side or until they are golden brown and reached an internal temperature of 63°C

Step 4: Remove the turkey legs onto a plate and let rest for 5 minutes.

Step 5: Serve the turkey legs warm.

23. TURKEY TENDERLOIN

Serve this mixed herb tenderloin with family and friends at your next celebratory dinner. They'll be impressed.

PREPARATION TIME: 10 MINUTES
COOKING TIME: 25 MINUTES
PER SERVING (4): KCAL: 253; FAT: 10.07G; CARBS: 0.81G; PROTEIN: 38.68G; SUGARS: 0.15G; FIBRE: 0.3G

INGRENKEDIENTS:

- 680 g turkey tenderloin
- 2 tbsp. olive oil
- Salt and black pepper to taste
- 1 tbsp. mixed herb seasoning

INSTRUCTIONS:

Step 1: Preheat the air fryer to 180°C.

Step 2: Rub the turkey on all sides with olive oil and season with salt, black pepper, and mixed herb seasoning.

Step 3: Put the turkey in the air fryer and bake for 20 to 25 minutes or until it reaches an internal temperature of 76°C.

Step 4: Remove the tenderloin onto a chopping board and let it rest for 5 to 10 minutes.

Step 5: Slice and serve warm.

24. VEAL PARMESAN

I often enjoy this veal dish for dinner. It packs much more flavour than chicken Parmesan, is more filling, and pairs well with baby potatoes and salad.

PREPARATION TIME: 10 MINUTES
COOKING TIME: 15 MINUTES
PER SERVING (4): KCAL: 395; FAT: 23G; CARBS: 16.27G; PROTEIN: 30.98; SUGARS: 3.41G; FIBRE: 1.7G

INGREDIENTS:

- 4 veal cutlets
- Salt and black pepper to taste
- 2 large eggs
- 110 g seasoned breadcrumbs
- 75 g grated Parmesan cheese
- 240 ml pasta sauce
- 225 g grated mozzarella cheese
- Chopped fresh basil for garnish

NSTRUCTIONS:

Step 1: Preheat the air fryer to 200°C.

Step 2: Season the veal on both sides with salt and black pepper.

Step 3: Crack the eggs into a bowl and lightly beat. On a plate, mix the breadcrumbs, half of the Parmesan cheese, and a pinch of black pepper.

Step 4: Dip the veal in the eggs and coat well with the breadcrumb mixture.

Step 5: Mist the air fryer with cooking spray and lay in the veal in the air fryer basket. Cook for 10 to 15 minutes or until the veal is golden brown and reaches an internal temperature of 63°C.

Step 6: Spoon the pasta sauce onto the veal and spread the mozzarella cheese on top. Bake for 1 more minute or until the cheese has melted.

Step 7: Remove the chicken onto a plate, garnish with basil, sprinkle on the remaining Parmesan, and serve warm with pasta.

25. VEGETABLE POT PIE

This creamy pot pie goes well around the dinner table and everyone who takes a bite will be pleased.

PREPARATION TIME: 15 MINUTES
COOKING TIME: 35 MINUTES
PER SERVING (4): KCAL: 807; FAT: 44.27G; CARBS: 88.79G; PROTEIN: 14.73G; SUGARS: 5.19G; FIBRE: 8.4G

INGRENKEDIENTS:

- 2 tbsp. olive oil
- 1 potato, peeled and finely diced
- 225 g sliced mushrooms
- 450 g frozen vegetable mix, type of choice
- Salt and black pepper to taste
- 75 g plain flour
- 360 ml vegetable stock
- 120 ml double cream
- 225 g peas
- 1 tbsp. chopped parsley
- 1 (400 g) refrigerated package pie crust, defrosted
- 1 large egg, beaten

INSTRUCTIONS:

Step 1: Heat the olive oil in a skillet over medium heat on a stove top and sauté the potato and mushrooms for 10 minutes or until they are tender. Add the frozen vegetable mix and sauté for 3 to 5 minutes or until warmed through. Add the garlic and cook for 1 minute or until fragrant. Season with salt and black pepper.

Step 2: Stir in the flour and cook for 1 to 2 minutes or until light brown. Stir in the vegetable stock and double cream. Let the sauce come to a soft boil and stir in the peas and parsley.

Step 3: Preheat the air fryer to 180°C.

Step 4: Spoon the sauce into a pie dish (with a good size for your air fryer) and cover the dish with the pastry. Crimp the edges to seal, trim off any excess, and brush the top with egg. Also, use a knife to cut 1 to 2 slits through the pastry.

Step 5: Place the dish in the air fryer and bake for 15 to 18 minutes or until the crust is golden brown and the filling is bubbly.

Step 6: Remove the dish from the air fryer and let it rest for 5 minutes.

Step 7: Serve warm.

SECTION 6.

VEGAN

**Don't Forget To Get The Color Images FREE!
Simply Scan The QR Code Below!**

Please scan the QR code below to access your bonus PDF with all 150 recipes with full coloured photos & beautiful designs alongside!

This is the only way we can get the recipes with coloured photos to you & keep the book as reasonably priced as possible.

Also, once downloaded you can take the PDF with you digitally wherever you go- meaning you can cook these recipes wherever you may be! (As long as you have an air fryer!)

We hope you enjoy and do let us know your feedback!

(INSERT QR CODE HERE)

STEP BY STEP Guide-

1. Open Your Phones (Or Any Device You Want The Book On) Back Camera. The Back Camera Is The One You use as if you are taking a picture of someone.
2. Simply point your Camera at the QR code and 'tap' the QR code with your finger to focus the camera.
3. A link / pop up will appear. Simply tap that (and make sure you have internet connection) and the FREE PDF containing all of the coloured images should appear.
4. Now you have access to these FOREVER. Simply 'Bookmark' The tab it opened on, or download the document and take wherever you want.
5. Repeat this on any device you want it on! (If you want it on a laptop, simply email the document to yourself!)

Any issues please email us at **vicandersonpublishing@gmail.com** and we will be happy to help!!

1. AVOCADO "EGG" ROLLS

Here, we get to make some fresh "egg" roll wrappers because I know how hard these are to find. Meanwhile, I ensure that the method is simple, so once they are ready, the filling becomes quite straightforward. Overall, these rolls are yummy.

PREPARATION TIME: 3 HOURS 20 MINUTES
COOKING TIME: 10 MINUTES
PER SERVING (4): KCAL: 826; FAT: 48.27G; CARBS: 87.43G; PROTEIN: 16G; SUGARS: 2.32G; FIBRE: 13.1G

INGRENKEDIENTS:

For the "egg" roll wrappers:
- 40 g flaxseed flour
- 200 g water
- 350 g plain flour
- 1/2 tsp. sea salt
- 100 g light olive oil
- 100 g water

For the filling:
- 3 avocados, halved, pitted, and peeled
- 75 g diced onion
- 110 g tomatoes, diced
- 2 tbsp. chopped fresh coriander
- Salt and black pepper to taste
- 1 lime, juiced

INSTRUCTIONS:

For the "egg" roll wrappers:

Step 1: In a small bowl, mix the flaxseed flour and water until smooth. Let sit for 5 minutes or until slimy in texture.

Step 2: In a large bowl, mix the plain flour, salt, olive oil, water, and flaxseed mixture. Mix until a dough comes together.

Step 3: Dust a working surface with flour, transfer the dough on top, and knead for about 5 minutes or until the dough is smooth, elastic, and not sticky. Put the dough in a bowl, cover it with a clean napkin, and let it rest in the fridge for 3 hours or overnight.

Step 4: Remove the dough from the fridge and divide it into 16 balls. Roll out each ball into a light sheet. These would be used as the wrappers.

For the filling:

Step 5: Preheat the air fryer to 200°C.

Step 6: Add the avocado to a bowl and use a fork to mash it until it is mostly smooth. Add the onion, tomatoes, coriander, salt, black pepper, and lime juice. Mix well.

Step 6: Divide the mixture onto the flour wrappers. Fold two opposite sides of the wrappers over the filling. Dip your finger in water and brush the edges of the other two sides with it. Fold these other sides over the filling and gently run your finger around the edges to seal.

Step 7: Grease the air fryer basket with cooking spray, lay in the rolls in a single layer and mist their tops with cooking spray. Air fry them for 5 minutes per side or until they are golden brown.

Step 8: Remove them onto a plate to cool slightly and serve warm.

2. BANANA AND CURRANT BREAD

This banana bread is so moist and features dotted currants all within for a classic bread look from the earlier days.

PREPARATION TIME: 15 MINUTES
COOKING TIME: 25 MINUTES
PER SERVING (4): KCAL: 860; FAT: 33.8G; CARBS: 128.49G; PROTEIN: 14.28G; SUGARS: 51.12G; FIBRE: 7G

INGREDIENTS:

For the flax egg:
- 30 g flaxseed flour
- 75 ml water

For the wet ingredients:
- 110 g melted vegan butter
- 170 g granulated sugar
- Prepared flax eggs
- 120 ml almond milk
- 1 tsp. vanilla extract
- 2 bananas, peeled and smoothly mashed
- 340 g plain flour
- 1 tsp. baking powder
- 1 tsp. salt
- 110 g currants

NSTRUCTIONS:

Step 1: Preheat the air fryer to 160°C.

For the flaxseed eggs:

Step 2: In a bowl, mix the flaxseed flour and water. Let it sit for 5 minutes or until the mixture is slimy.

For the batter:

Step 3: In a large bowl, whisk the melted vegan butter, sugar, flax eggs, almond milk, vanilla, and mashed bananas.

Step 4: Sift the plain flour, baking powder, and salt into the wet mixture and whisk until smooth batter forms.

Step 5: Fold in the currants.

Step 6: Grease a loaf pan (safe for your air fryer) with vegan butter and pour the bread batter into it. Use a spoon to level the top evenly.

Step 7: Place the pan in the air fryer and bake for 20 to 25 minutes or until a toothpick inserted into the bread pulls out clean.

Step 8: Remove the pan from the air fryer and let the bread cool in it for 10 minutes. After, transfer it to a wire rack and let it cool completely.

Step 9: Slice the bread and enjoy.

The UK Air Fryer Cookbook for Beginners

3. BATTERED TOFU SLABS

This vegan beer-battered tofu will leave you super impressed. Even if you aren't vegan, you just might prefer this version to the many other battered competitors.

PREPARATION TIME: 15 MINUTES
COOKING TIME: 10 MINUTES
PER SERVING (4): KCAL: 346; FAT: 7.93G; CARBS: 49.95G; PROTEIN: 17.45G; SUGARS: 0.77G; FIBRE: 2.6G

INGREDIENTS:

For the flaxseed egg:
- 1 tbsp. flaxseed flour
- 40 ml water

For the battered tofu:
- 400 g plain flour
- 30 g corn flour
- 1/2 tsp. baking soda
- 175 ml vegan beer
- 1/2 tsp. paprika
- 1 tsp. salt
- A pinch of black pepper
- 450 g extra firm tofu, pressed

INSTRUCTIONS:

Step 1: Preheat the air fryer to 180°C.

For the flaxseed egg:

Step 2: In a bowl, mix the flaxseed flour and water until smooth. Let it sit for 5 minutes or until slimy.

For the battered tofu:

Step 2: In a bowl, mix 1 cup of plain flour, corn flour, baking soda, and vegan beer until smooth. Pour the flaxseed egg onto a plate and on another plate, mix the remaining flour, paprika, salt, and black pepper.

Step 3: Pat the tofu dry with paper towels and cut into 4 cm thick slabs. Dredge the tofu in the dry flour mix, then dip them in the flax egg, and then in the vegan beer batter.

Step 4: Line the air fryer with parchment paper, mist it with cooking spray, and lay the battered tofu on top. Mist the top also with cooking spray.

Step 5: Air fry for 3 to 5 minutes per side or until the tofu is golden brown and warmed through.

Step 6: Plate the tofu and serve warm.

4. BLACK BEAN BURGERS

Yes to bean burgers as they are sumptuous and oh-so delicious. These burgers are superfast to make so you can have lunch in little time.

PREPARATION TIME: 10 MINUTES
COOKING TIME: 12 MINUTES
PER SERVING (4): KCAL: 604; FAT: 19.53; CARBS: 89.99G; PROTEIN: 18.78G; SUGARS: 23.21G; FIBRE: 14.1G

INGREDIENTS:

- 680 g canned and drained black beans
- ¼ cup onion, diced
- 1 tsp. minced garlic
- Salt and black pepper to taste
- 1 tsp. onion powder
- 1 tsp. garlic powder
- 225 g vegan breadcrumbs
- 4 vegan burger buns, split
- Vegan ketchup, store-bought
- 4 tomato slices
- 4 red onion slices
- 4 lettuce leaves

INSTRUCTIONS:

Step 1: Preheat the air fryer to 180°C.

Step 2: In a bowl, slightly mash the black beans and mix with the onion, garlic, salt, black pepper, onion powder, garlic powder, and vegan breadcrumbs. Form 4 patties out of the mixture.

Step 3: Mist the air fryer with cooking spray, place in the bean patties, and mist their tops with cooking spray. Air fry for 5 to 6 minutes per side.

Step 4: Remove the bean patties onto a plate and toast the burger buns in the air fryer for 1 minute. Take them out after.

Step 5: On the bottom parts of the burger buns, spread some vegan ketchup and top with one bean burger each. Top with one each of the tomato slice, red onion, and lettuce leaf. Cover with the top buns and serve.

5. CARROT MUG CAKE

Enjoy this mug cake for breakfast. On some days, I like to top it with coconut cream for a better depth of flavour.

PREPARATION TIME: 10 MINUTES
COOKING TIME: 8 MINUTES
PER SERVING (1): KCAL: 420; FAT: 15.7G; CARBS: 65.39G; PROTEIN: 6.55G; SUGARS: 25.08G; FIBRE: 5G

INGREDIENTS:

For the flaxseed egg:
- 1 tbsp. flaxseed flour
- 40 ml water

For the mug cake:
- 1 tbsp. unsalted vegan butter, melted
- 45 g plain flour
- 1/2 tsp. baking powder
- A pinch of cinnamon powder
- 25 g granulated sugar
- 1 small carrot, finely grated

INSTRUCTIONS:

Step 1: Preheat the air fryer to 175°C.

For the flaxseed egg:

Step 2: In a bowl, mix the flaxseed flour with water until smooth. Let it sit for 5 minutes or until it is slimy.

For the mug cake:

Step 2: Whisk the flaxseed egg with the vegan butter. Add the flour, baking powder, cinnamon powder, and sugar. Whisk until smooth and fold in the carrots.

Step 3: Put the mug in the air fryer and bake for 5 to 8 minutes or until the cake sets when you test it with a toothpick.

Step 4: Take out the mug, let it cool for about 5 minutes, and enjoy.

6. CAULIFLOWER WINGS

These cauliflower wings are spicy, as they should be. They cook tender with a little crunch to them and would pair well with celery sticks.

PREPARATION TIME: 10 MINUTES
COOKING TIME: 10 MINUTES
PER SERVING (4): KCAL: 235; FAT: 7.19G; CARBS: 38G;.78 PROTEIN: 5.8G; SUGARS: 14.62G; FIBRE: 3G

INGREDIENTS:

- 120 ml soy milk
- 120 ml water
- 170 g plain flour
- 1 tsp. onion powder
- 1 tsp. garlic powder
- 1 tsp. smoked paprika
- Salt and black pepper to taste
- 1 head of cauliflower, cut into florets
- 30 g vegan butter
- 240 ml hot sauce
- 60 ml pure maple syrup
- Chopped green onions for garnish

INSTRUCTIONS:

Step 1: Preheat the air fryer to 180°C and line the air fryer basket with parchment paper.

Step 2: In a bowl, mix the soy milk and water. Whisk in the flour, onion powder, garlic powder, paprika, salt, and black pepper until smooth.

Step 3: Dip the cauliflower florets in the batter to coat well and place them in the air fryer basket. Mist them with cooking spray.

Step 4: Air fry for 3 to 5 minutes per side or until they are golden brown and tender.

Step 5: Remove the cauliflower into a bowl.

Step 6: In a small bowl, mix the vegan butter, hot sauce, and maple syrup until smooth. Drizzle the mixture over the cauliflower and toss until they are well coated with the sauce.

Step 7: Garnish with green onions and serve warm.

7. CHICKPEA AND CAULIFLOWER TACOS

Bite into these hearty tacos, take a second one, and repeat until you are full.

PREPARATION TIME: 10 MINUTES
COOKING TIME: 10 MINUTES
PER SERVING (4): KCAL: 850; FAT: 49.82G; CARBS: 89.55G; PROTEIN: 19.63G; SUGARS: 12.26G; FIBRE: 19G

INGREDIENTS:

- 900 g cauliflower florets, cut into bite-sized bites
- 1 (425 g) can chickpeas, drained and rinsed
- 2 tbsp. olive oil
- 2 tbsp. taco seasoning

For serving:

- 8 small vegan tortillas
- 2 avocados, sliced
- 4 cups cabbage, shredded
- Vegan coconut yoghurt for topping

INSTRUCTIONS:

Step 1: Preheat the air fryer to 180°C.

Step 2: In a bowl, toss the cauliflower, chickpeas, olive oil, and taco seasoning until well coated.

Step 3: Add the mixture to the air fryer basket and cook for 8 to 10 minutes while shaking the basket halfway. When the cauliflower is tender and the chickpeas are warmed through, they are ready.

Step 4: To serve, spoon the cauliflower and chickpeas into the tortillas and top with the avocado, cabbage, and vegan coconut yoghurt.

Step 5: Serve right away.

8. CHICKPEA BALLS

I love to make these chickpea balls in batches as they come in handy for many servings. You can serve them with pasta, throw them into stew, snack on them, or add them to salads, The list goes on.

PREPARATION TIME: 18 TO 24 HOURS + 45 MINUTES
COOKING TIME: 16 MINUTES
PER SERVING (4): KCAL: 402; FAT: 6.42G; CARBS: 68.06G; PROTEIN: 21.58G; SUGARS: 11.66G; FIBRE: 13.4G

INGREDIENTS:

- 400 g dried chickpeas
- 1 small onion, chopped
- 5 garlic cloves, chopped
- 225 g chopped fresh parsley
- 110 g chopped fresh coriander
- 2 tsp. ground cumin
- 2 tsp. ground coriander
- A pinch of cayenne pepper to taste
- 1 tsp. baking powder
- Salt and black pepper to taste

INSTRUCTIONS:

Step 1: Preheat the air fryer to 190°C.

Step 2: Soak the chickpeas in water for 18 to 24 hours. Drain and rinse after.

Step 3: Transfer the chickpeas to a food processor and add the remaining ingredients. Process until smooth. Pour the batter into a bowl and refrigerate for 30 minutes.

Step 4: Using a cookie scoop, form as many balls from the mixture as possible and mist them with cooking spray.

Step 5: Put the chickpea balls in the air fryer basket and air fry for 5 to 8 minutes per side or until they are golden brown.

Step 6: Remove the chickpea balls onto a plate and serve warm.

9. CORIANDER AND SWEET POTATO PATTIES

The aroma that hits you from these patties would leave you speechless for a moment. Coriander makes many things better and does not disappoint in these sweet potato patties either.

PREPARATION TIME: 15 MINUTES
COOKING TIME: 12 MINUTES
PER SERVING (4): KCAL: 164; FAT: 9.23G; CARBS: 17.82G; PROTEIN: 4.3G; SUGARS: 5.21G; FIBRE: 4.5G

INGRENKEDIENTS:

For the flaxseed eggs:
- 2 tbsp. flaxseed flour
- 80 ml water

For the patties:
- 2 sweet potatoes, peeled and pre-boiled
- Prepared flaxseed eggs
- 110 g almond flour
- 60 g diced onions
- A pinch of ground coriander
- 1/2 tsp. salt
- 1/2 tsp. ground black pepper
- 2 tsp. olive oil
- 1 tbsp. chopped fresh coriander, plus extra for garnish

INSTRUCTIONS:

Step 1: Preheat the air fryer to 190°C.

For the flaxseed eggs:

Step 2: In a bowl, mix the flaxseed flour and water. Let it sit for 5 minutes or until the mixture is slimy.

For the patties:

Step 3: Mash the sweet potatoes in a bowl and add the flaxseed eggs and remaining ingredients. Mix well and form four patties from the mixture.

Step 4: Mist the air fryer basket with cooking spray and place the patties in it in a single layer.

Step 5: Air fry for 5 to 6 minutes per side or until the sweet potato patties are golden brown and compacted.

Step 6: Remove them onto a plate, garnish with coriander, and serve with your favourite dipping sauce.

10. COURGETTE CORN PATTIES

I call these patties bite-worthy as they include soft bits of corn kernels and a refreshing parsley flavour.

PREPARATION TIME: 45 MINUTES
COOKING TIME: 16 MINUTES
PER SERVING (4): KCAL: 64; FAT: 1.1G; CARBS: 12.93G; PROTEIN: 2.25G; SUGARS: 1.32G; FIBRE: 1.8G

INGREDIENTS:

For the flaxseed egg:
- 1 tbsp. flaxseed flour
- 40 ml water

For the fritters:
- 2 medium courgettes
- ½ small onion
- 225 g canned and drained sweetcorn
- 30 g plain flour
- 1 tsp. onion powder
- 1 tsp. garlic powder
- 1/2 tsp. dried parsley
- Salt and black pepper to taste

NSTRUCTIONS:

For the flaxseed eggs:

Step 1: In a bowl, mix the flaxseed flour and water. Let it sit for 5 minutes or until the mixture is slimy.

For the fritters:

Step 2: Into a bowl, coarsely grate the courgettes and onion. Add the corn, flaxseed egg, plain flour, onion powder, garlic powder, parsley, salt, and black pepper. Mix well and form 4 patties from the mixture. Place them in the fridge for 30 minutes.

Step 3: Preheat the air fryer to 190°C.

Step 4: Grease the air fryer basket with cooking spray and arrange the fritters in it in a single layer. Mist their tops with a little cooking spray.

Step 5: Air fry the fritters for 6 to 8 minutes per side or until golden brown and compacted.

Step 6: Remove them onto a plate and serve with your favourite dipping sauce.

The UK Air Fryer Cookbook for Beginners

11. CURRIED CHICKPEA POTATO JACKETS

A little piece goes a long way as these potatoes are pretty loaded and delicious.

PREPARATION TIME: 10 MINUTES
COOKING TIME: 25 MINUTES
PER SERVING (4): KCAL: 633; FAT: 23.37G; CARBS: 95.16G; PROTEIN: 16.57G; SUGARS: 7.57G; FIBRE: 20G

INGREDIENTS:

- 2 (425 g) cans chickpeas, drained and rinsed
- 2 tbsp. coconut oil
- 2 tbsp. curry powder
- Salt and black pepper to taste
- 4 medium potatoes
- 2 tbsp. vegan butter, melted
- 1 tbsp. hot sauce
- 1 avocado, halved, pitted, and sliced
- Fresh parsley for garnish

INSTRUCTIONS:

Step 1: Preheat the air fryer to 190°C.

Step 2: Cut the potatoes in halves without cutting them all the way through. Drizzle them with 1 tbsp. of coconut oil and season with salt and black pepper.

Step 3: Place them in the air fryer and bake for 20 to 25 minutes or until the potatoes are tender and their skins still intact.

Step 4: Remove the potatoes onto a plate and cool slightly.

Step 5: Meanwhile, in a bowl, combine the chickpeas, remaining coconut oil, curry powder, salt, and black pepper. Toss well.

Step 6: Spread the chickpeas in the air fryer basket and bake for 6 to 8 minutes while shaking the basket halfway until they are golden brown and warmed through.

Step 7: While the chickpeas cook, use a fork to carefully scoop out the potatoes flesh into a bowl without damaging the skins.

Step 8: Spoon the chickpeas onto the potato flesh. Add the melted vegan butter and hot sauce, and mix well.

Step 9: Spoon the chickpeas and potatoes into the potato skins and top with the avocados.

Step 10: Garnish with parsley and serve warm.

12. FRIED TEMPEH WITH PEANUT SAUCE

You can make these crispy tempeh cubes and enjoy them as a snack with peanut sauce. Also, they'll be great over spinach salad drizzled with the same peanut sauce.

PREPARATION TIME: 10 MINUTES
COOKING TIME: 15 MINUTES
PER SERVING (4): KCAL: 352; FAT: 26.5G; CARBS: 17.85G; PROTEIN: 16.67G; SUGARS: 7.24G; FIBRE: 2.1G

INGREDIENTS:

For the tempeh:

- 1 (225 g) package tempeh, cut into 3 cm cubes
- 1 tbsp. avocado oil
- 1 tsp. toasted sesame oil
- 1 tbsp. soy sauce
- 1 tsp. garlic powder
- Salt to taste, if needed

For the peanut sauce:

- 120 ml salted creamy peanut butter
- 1 tbsp. soy sauce
- 1 tsp. chilli garlic sauce
- 2 tbsp. pure maple syrup
- 2 tbsp. fresh lime juice
- 60 ml water to thin

INSTRUCTIONS:

For the tempeh:

Step 1: Add the tempeh to a bowl and top with the oils, soy sauce, garlic powder, and salt if needed. Mix well and let it sit to marinate for 10 minutes.

Step 2: Preheat the air fryer to 190°C.

Step 3: Place the tofu in the air fryer basket and bake for 7 to 8 minutes per side or until golden brown.

For the peanut sauce:

Step 4: As the tempeh cooks, in a bowl, mix the peanut butter, soy sauce, chilli garlic sauce, lime juice, and water until smooth and coats the back of the spoon easily.

Step 5: Remove the tempeh onto a servicing platter when it is ready and serve with the peanut sauce. Serve warm.

13. GARLIC MUSHROOMS

By simply tossing mushrooms with garlic olive oil, you enhance their tastes as a mouth-watering side dish for grilled tofu.

PREPARATION TIME: 10 MINUTES
COOKING TIME: 12 MINUTES
PER SERVING (4): KCAL: 42; FAT: 3.21G; CARBS: 2.23G; PROTEIN: 1.96G; SUGARS: 1.14G; FIBRE: 0.7G

INGRENKEDIENTS:

- 225 g sliced mushrooms, washed and dried
- 1 tbsp. olive oil
- 1 tsp. soy sauce
- ½ tsp. garlic powder
- Salt and black pepper to taste
- 1 tbsp. chopped fresh parsley

INSTRUCTIONS:

Step 1: Preheat the air fryer to 190°C.

Step 2: In a bowl, combine the mushrooms, olive oil, soy sauce, garlic powder, salt, and black pepper. Toss well.

Step 3: Add the mushrooms to the air fryer basket and cook for 10 to 12 minutes or until the mushrooms are tender.

Step 4: Spoon the mushrooms onto a serving platter and garnish with parsley.

Step 5: Serve warm.

14. GRILLED BOK CHOY

Bok choy has a punchy flavour that I love to add to soups. On other days, I roast them lightly with sesame oil as a delicacy with quinoa or rice with maple glazed tofu.

PREPARATION TIME: 10 MINUTES
COOKING TIME: 6 MINUTES
PER SERVING (4): KCAL: 36; FAT: 1.07G; CARBS: 5.69G; PROTEIN: 2.62G; SUGARS: 1.42G; FIBRE: 2.5G

INGREDIENTS:

- 4 baby bok choy
- 1 tsp. sesame oil
- 1/2 tsp. garlic powder
- Salt and black pepper to taste
- Sesame seeds for garnish

NSTRUCTIONS:

Step 1: Preheat the air fryer to 185°C.

Step 2: Slice the bok choy in halves and rinse well. Pat them dry and then put them in a bowl. Add the sesame oil, garlic powder, salt, and black pepper. Use your hands to rub the seasoning well all over them.

Step 3: Place the bok choy in the air fryer and cook for 3 minutes per side or until they are golden brown and tender.

Step 4: Put the bok choy on a plate and serve warm.

15. HASSELBACK POTATOES WITH HERB VINAIGRETTE

These potatoes bake so pretty and the herb vinaigrette soaks into the flesh for such delicious bites.

PREPARATION TIME: 10 MINUTES
COOKING TIME: 25 MINUTES
PER SERVING (4): KCAL: 376; FAT: 23.22G; CARBS: 39.55G; PROTEIN: 5G; SUGARS: 1.36G; FIBRE: 3G

INGREDIENTS:

- 4 medium russet potatoes
- Salt and black pepper to taste
- 110 g butter, melted
- 60 ml fresh lemon juice
- 1 tsp. chopped fresh thyme
- 1 tsp. chopped fresh parsley
- 1 tsp. chopped fresh rosemary
- 3 garlic cloves, minced

INSTRUCTIONS:

Step 1: Preheat the air fryer to 200°C.

Step 2: Thinly slice the potatoes towards the base but leave about 1 cm of the base intact. Season the potatoes with salt and black pepper.

Step 3: In a bowl, mix the butter, lemon juice, thyme, parsley, rosemary, and garlic. Brush the mixture on the potatoes.

Step 4: Place the air fryer in the air fryer and bake for 20 to 25 minutes or until the potatoes are golden brown and tender.

Step 5: Remove them onto a plate and garnish with parsley. Serve warm.

16. KALE AND POTATO NUGGETS

You can enjoy these nuggets with tempeh, roasted chickpeas, or your favourite dipping sauce.

PREPARATION TIME: 10 MINUTES
COOKING TIME: 12 MINUTES
PER SERVING (4): KCAL: 80; FAT: 1.43G; CARBS: 15.55G; PROTEIN: 1.43G; SUGARS: 1.9G; FIBRE: 1.6G

INGREDIENTS:

- 450 g mashed potatoes with vegan butter
- 900 g chopped kale
- 1 tsp. olive oil
- 1 garlic clove, minced
- 1/2 tsp. salt
- 2 tbsp. almond milk
- Salt and black pepper

INSTRUCTIONS:

Step 1: Preheat the air fryer to 185°C.

Step 2: In a bowl, mix the potatoes, kale, olive oil, garlic, almond milk, salt, and black pepper. Form 8 balls from the mixture.

Step 3: Place them in the air fryer and bake for 10 to 12 minutes or until they are golden brown and compacted.

Step 4: Remove them onto a plate and serve with your favourite dipping sauce.

17. MARINATED CAULIFLOWER WITH WATERCRESS PUREE

Why watercress puree? Because it gives the cauliflower some needed peppery hints to complement it. As well, it is a pretty presentation to behold while enhancing the aroma of the spiced cauliflower.

PREPARATION TIME: 20 MINUTES
COOKING TIME: 10 MINUTES
PER SERVING (4): KCAL: 647; FAT: 56.04G; CARBS: 32.47G; PROTEIN: 15.04G; SUGARS: 11.67G; FIBRE: 13.3G

INGRENKEDIENTS:

For the marinated cauliflower:
- 1 cauliflower head
- 1 tbsp. olive oil
- A pinch of curry powder
- 1/2 tsp. smoked paprika
- 1/2 tsp. salt
- A pinch of ground black pepper

For the watercress puree:
- 150 g watercress
- 45 ml olive oil
- A pinch of salt

INSTRUCTIONS:

For the marinated cauliflower:

Step 1: Stand the cauliflower and cut into 4 slabs from the top to the bottom. Put the slabs aside.

Step 2: In a bowl, mix the olive oil, curry powder, paprika, salt, and black pepper. Brush the mixture on both sides of the cauliflower and let it sit for 10 minutes to marinate.

Step 3: Preheat the air fryer to 190ºC.

Step 4: Place the cauliflower slabs in the air fryer basket and cook for 8 to 10 minutes while flipping them halfway until they are golden brown and tender. You may need to do this process in batches.

For the watercress puree:

Step 5: Add the watercress puree, olive oil, and salt to a blender. Blend until smooth.

Step 6: Plate the cauliflower when ready and dot the watercress puree on them.

Step 7: Serve warm.

18. MUSHROOM HAND PIES

Make a couple of these thyme-seasoned mushroom hand pies for a quick snack for your day out.

PREPARATION TIME: 15 MINUTES
COOKING TIME: 22 MINUTES
PER SERVING (4): KCAL: 949; FAT: 57.17G; CARBS: 102.77G; PROTEIN: 57.17G; SUGARS: 0.06G; FIBRE: 3.7G

INGREDIENTS:

- 1 tbsp. olive oil
- 225 g sliced white mushrooms
- 1 garlic clove, minced
- 1/2 tsp. dried thyme
- 1 tbsp. soy sauce
- Black pepper to taste
- 2 (400 g) refrigerated package pie crusts, defrosted
- 1 tbsp. vegan butter, melted

INSTRUCTIONS:

Step 1: Preheat the air fryer to 175ºC.

Step 2: Heat the olive oil in a skillet and sauté the mushrooms for 10 to 12 minutes or until the liquid has evaporated and is tender. Stir in the garlic and thyme, and cook for 1 minute or until fragrant. Season with the soy sauce and black pepper.

Step 3: Lay out the pie crusts on a clean flat surface and cut out four 12 cm diameter circles.

Step 4: Divide the mushroom mixture on one half of each of the circles and fold the empty half over the filling. Using a fork, crimp the edges to seal the pie. Brush the butter on top of them.

Step 5: Mist the air fryer basket with cooking spray and place two pies in it.

Step 6: Bake for 10 minutes or until the crust is golden brown and the mushroom is warm within.

Step 7: Remove the hand pies onto a wire rack to cool while you bake the others.

Step 8: Serve them warm or cold.

19. PERSIMMON, TOFU, AND PEPPER SKEWERS

You may not often see persimmons roasted with tofu and that is unique but delicious. Each bite bursts with sweet and mild richness and the sweet aromas that red bell peppers offer.

PREPARATION TIME: 1 HOUR 10 MINUTES
COOKING TIME: 10 MINUTES
PER SERVING (4): KCAL: 267; FAT: 16.22G; CARBS: 18.26G; PROTEIN: 15.81G; SUGARS: 4.33G; FIBRE: 2.4G

INGRENKEDIENTS:

- 8 metal skewers (with good length for your air fryer)
- 4 persimmons, deseeded and cut into 2 cm cubes
- 450 g extra firm tofu, pressed and cut into 2 cm cubes
- 2 red bell peppers, deseeded and cut into 2 cm cubes
- 120 ml soy sauce
- 1 tsp. pure maple syrup
- 1 tsp. sesame oil
- 75 ml rice vinegar
- 2 tbsp. olive oil
- 2 garlic cloves, minced
- 2 tbsp. white sesame seeds for garnish

INSTRUCTIONS:

Step 1: On the skewers, alternately thread the persimmons, tofu, and bell peppers.

Step 2: In a bowl, mix the soy sauce, maple syrup, sesame oil, rice vinegar, olive oil, and garlic. Brush the mixture all over the skewers and let them marinate in the fridge for 1 hour.

Step 3: Preheat the air fryer to 190°C.

Step 4: Place the skewers in the air fryer basket and cook for 3 to 5 minutes per side or until they are golden brown.

Step 5: Remove them onto a plate and garnish with sesame seeds. Serve warm.

20. ROASTED POTATO WEDGES WITH VEGAN MAPLE MUSTARD MAYO

Traditionally, roasted potato wedges pair with mayonnaise, so we make some plant-based version here that has a sweet note to it.

PREPARATION TIME: 10 MINUTES
COOKING TIME: 20 MINUTES
PER SERVING (4): KCAL: 636; FAT: 60.08G; CARBS: 24.45G; PROTEIN: 2.97G; SUGARS: 4.42G; FIBRE: 1.8G

INGREDIENTS:

For the potato wedges:

- 2 medium Russet potatoes, well-scrubbed, peeled, and cut into wedges
- 2 tbsp. olive oil
- A pinch of garlic powder
- 1/2 tsp. paprika
- Salt and black pepper to taste

For the vegan maple mustard mayo:

- 120 ml soy milk
- 240 ml sunflower oil
- 1 tbsp. yellow mustard
- 1 tbsp. pure maple syrup
- 1 tbsp. fresh lemon juice or to taste
- Salt and black pepper to taste

NSTRUCTIONS:

For the potato wedges:

Step 1: Preheat the air fryer to 200°C.

Step 2: In a bowl, toss the potatoes with the olive oi, garlic powder, paprika, salt, and black pepper.

Step 3: Put the potatoes in the air fryer basket and air fry for 18 to 20 minutes or until golden brown and tender. Meanwhile, shake the basket once or twice during cooking.

Step 4: Remove the potatoes onto a platter.

For the vegan maple mustard mayo:

Step 5: In a blender, add the soy milk, sunflower oil, yellow mustard, maple syrup, and lemon juice. Blend until smooth and thick. Season with salt and black pepper.

Step 6: Serve the potato wedges with vegan maple mustard mayo.

21. SIMPLE ALL-ROUNDER TOFU

This tofu is what you'll need for nearly any recipe. So, keep this note close by.

PREPARATION TIME: 10 MINUTES
COOKING TIME: 12 MINUTES
PER SERVING (4): KCAL: 168; FAT: 13.42G; CARBS: 2.91G; PROTEIN: 11.92G; SUGARS: 0.61G; FIBRE: 0.5G

INGRENKEDIENTS:

- 450 g extra-firm tofu, pressed and cut into cubes or slabs
- 2 tbsp. soy sauce
- 1 tbsp. olive oil
- 1 tbsp. toasted sesame oil
- 1 garlic clove, minced

INSTRUCTIONS:

Step 1: Add the tofu to a bowl. In a small bowl, mix the soy sauce, olive oil, sesame oil, and garlic. Pour the mixture over the tofu and mix well. Let it marinate for 10 minutes.

Step 2: Preheat the air fryer to 175°C.

Step 3: Place the tofu in the air fryer and cook for 5 to 6 minutes per side or until golden brown.

Step 4: Plate the tofu and serve it warm with as many sides as desired.

22. SOYA NUGGETS WITH ROASTED LEMONS

When I got introduced to soya nuggets, I was clueless with regards to what to do with them. And then, I started exploring breading them and using them as salad complements. They have since been one of my best pairs with salads. Here, I combine them with rocket and some roasted lemons.

PREPARATION TIME: 10 MINUTES
COOKING TIME: 10 MINUTES
PER SERVING (4): KCAL: 240; FAT: 2.52G; CARBS: 33.82G; PROTEIN: 23.45G; SUGARS: 1.29G; FIBRE: 4.7G

INGREDIENTS:

- 110 g soya pieces
- 1.4 L boiling water
- 1 tbsp. flaxseed flour
- 40 ml cold water
- 110 g fine-ground corn flour
- 1 tsp. onion powder
- 1 tsp. garlic powder
- 1 tbsp. smoked paprika
- 110 g nutritional yeast
- Salt and black pepper to taste
- 4 lemons, halved
- Rocket leaves for serving

NSTRUCTIONS:

Step 1: Preheat the air fryer to 190°C.

Step 2: Add the soya pieces to a bowl and pour on the boiling water. Let them soak for 10 to 15 minutes. After, drain the soya pieces and press out as much water out of them.

Step 3: Meanwhile, mix the flaxseed flour and water in a bowl. Let it sit for 5 minutes or until it is slimy. On a plate, mix the corn flour, onion powder, garlic powder, smoked paprika, nutritional yeast, salt, and black pepper.

Step 4: Dip the soya pieces in the flaxseed mixture (flaxseed egg) and then coat in the corn flour mixture until well-coated.

Step 5: Mist the air fryer with cooking spray, put the soya pieces in it, and mist it with cooking spray. Place a trivet (with good size for your air fryer) over the soya pieces and place the lemons on top.

Step 6: Cook for 8 to 10 minutes or until the soya pieces are golden brown, while turning them half way.

Step 7: Remove the lemons and soya pieces onto a plate and serve with rocket.

23. SUPREME CRUNCHWRAP

I call these wraps the perfect work-from-home meal. It is not fussy, packs a good amount of filling, has the perfect crunch, and gives you the ideal feeling of working out of a coffee shop.

PREPARATION TIME: 10 MINUTES
COOKING TIME: 8 MINUTES
PER SERVING (4): KCAL: 359; FAT: 21.41G; CARBS: 29.49G; PROTEIN: 13.12G; SUGARS: 3.16G; FIBRE: 3.1G

INGREDIENTS:

- 4 large flour tortillas
- 110 g shredded green cabbage
- 60 ml vegan pesto, store-bought
- 4 vegan cheddar cheese slices
- 60 ml tomato sauce
- 1 (425 g) cans black beans, drained, rinsed, and mashed

INSTRUCTIONS:

Step 1: Preheat the air fryer to 200°C.

Step 2: Lay out each tortilla and divide the cabbage on top. Spoon the pesto in the centre, top with the vegan cheddar cheese, tomato sauce, and black beans. Wrap the tortillas over the filling.

Step 3: Mist the air fryer basket with cooking spray, place in the wraps, and mist with cooking spray. Bake for 2 to 4 minutes per side or until the tortillas are golden brown and crispy.

Step 4: Remove them onto a plate, slice in half, and serve warm.

24. VEGAN AUBERGINE "PARMESAN"

This aubergine "Parmesan" is a plant-based Parmesan that gives the aubergine slices so much life and character.

PREPARATION TIME: 15 MINUTES
COOKING TIME: 8 MINUTES
PER SERVING (4): KCAL: 203; FAT: 10.2G; CARBS: 17.12G; PROTEIN: 11.61G; SUGARS: 4.13G; FIBRE: 3.5G

INGREDIENTS:

- 1 tbsp. flaxseed flour
- 40 ml water
- 4 thick aubergine slices
- 110 g vegan breadcrumbs
- 1/2 tsp. dried herb mix
- 75 g grated vegan Parmesan cheese
- Salt and black pepper to taste
- 60 ml tomato sauce
- 225 g grated vegan mozzarella cheese
- Chopped fresh basil for garnish

INSTRUCTIONS:

Step 1: Preheat the air fryer to 180°C.

Step 2: In a bowl, make the flaxseed egg by mixing the flaxseed flour and water. Let it sit for 5 minutes or until it is slimy.

Step 3: On a plate, mix the breadcrumbs, herb mix, vegan Parmesan cheese, salt, and black pepper.

Step 4: Dip the aubergine in the flaxseed egg and then coat well with the breadcrumb mixture.

Step 5: Mist the air fryer with cooking spray and place in the air fryer basket. Mist the top with cooking spray and bake for 3 to 4 minutes per side or until golden brown and the aubergines are tender.

Step 6: Spoon the tomato sauce onto the aubergines and spread the vegan mozzarella cheese on top. Bake for 1 more minute or until the cheese has melted.

Step 7: Remove the aubergines, garnish with basil, and serve warm.

25. VEGAN BEAN BALLS

These bean balls tend to offer softer bites. I particularly like to toss them in tomato sauce and serve them over pasta with some basil.

PREPARATION TIME: 10 MINUTES
COOKING TIME: 10 MINUTES
PER SERVING (4): KCAL: 224; FAT: 11.9G; CARBS: 23.08G; PROTEIN: 8.44G; SUGARS: 4.31G; FIBRE: 4.5G

INGREDIENTS:

- 225 g cooked quinoa, cooled
- 1 (425 g) can black beans, rinsed and drained
- 2 tbsp. avocado oil
- 110 g diced shallot
- 3 garlic cloves, minced
- 1 tbsp. soy sauce
- 1 tbsp. fresh oregano
- 1/2 tsp. red pepper flakes
- Salt and black pepper to taste
- 2 tbsp. tomato paste
- 110 g vegan Parmesan cheese, plus extra for vegan Parmesan cheese
- 45 g chopped fresh parsley

INSTRUCTIONS:

Step 1: Preheat the air fryer to 180°C.

Step 2: In a bowl, add the quinoa, black beans, avocado oil, shallot, garlic, soy sauce, oregano, red pepper flakes, salt, black pepper, tomato paste, vegan Parmesan cheese, and parsley. Mix well and form 8 balls out of the mixture.

Step 3: Mist the air fryer basket with cooking spray, add the bean balls, and mist with cooking spray.

Step 4: Air fry for 5 minutes per side or until golden brown and compacted.

Step 5: Remove the vegan bean balls onto a plate and serve warm.

WRAPPING UP

The air fryer is certainly worth the investment for any beginner cook. It is a good choice that offers you versatility across cooking functions. As you have seen in these recipes, I explore the different ways to use the air fryer while creating a collection of mouth-watering dishes for everyday consumption.

All 150 recipes are created with you in mind as you familiarise yourself with using the air fryer. They are easy to make but with a few options that are slightly challenging to help you build on your expertise.

Meanwhile, if you haven't gotten an air fryer yet, I hope these recipes are enough inspiration for you to get one.

I am always delighted to create tasty foods that can help beginner cooks like you reduce unhealthy takeaways as you expose yourself to eating nutritiously. And the air fryer helps well with this.

I hope you've enjoyed the recipes as much as I loved making them. It is my desire that they'll be regulars in your home as you share with others too.

Printed in Great Britain
by Amazon